Teaching
Thinking Skills

Also available in the Key Debates in Educational Policy Series

Special Educational Needs, Mary Warnock and Brahm Norwich, edited by Lorella Terzi

Educational Equality, Harry Brighouse, Kenneth R. Howe and James Tooley, edited by Graham Haydon

Teaching Thinking Skills

2nd Edition

Stephen Johnson
and Harvey Siegel

Edited by
Christopher Winch

Key Debates in Educational Policy

continuum

Continuum International Publishing Group
The Tower Building   80 Maiden Lane
11 York Road   Suite 704
London, SE1 7NX   New York, NY 10038

www.continuumbooks.com

© Christopher Winch; © Part 1, Stephen Johnson; © Part 2 Harvey Siegel 2010

All rights reserved. No part of this publication may be reproduced or transmitted in any form or by any means, electronic or mechanical, including photocopying, recording, or any information storage or retrieval system, without prior permission in writing from the publishers.

Stephen Johnson and Harvey Siegel have asserted their right under the Copyright, Designs and Patents Act, 1988, to be identified as Authors of this work.

British Library Cataloguing-in-Publication Data
A catalogue record for this book is available from the British Library.

ISBN: 978-1-4411-8656-0 (paperback)

Library of Congress Cataloging-in-Publication Data
Johnson, Stephen.
Teaching thinking skills/Stephen Johnson and Harvey Siegel; edited by Christopher Winch.
   p. cm.–(Key debates in educational policy)
Includes bibliographical references and index.
ISBN   978-1-4411-8656-0 (pbk.)
1. Thought and thinking–Study and teaching. I. Siegel, Harvey, 1952- II. Winch, Christopher. III. Title.

LB1590.3.J65 2010
370.15'2–dc22   2009045433

Typeset by Newgen Imaging Systems Pvt Ltd., Chennai, India
Printed and bound in Great Britain by the MPG Books Group

Contents

Series Editor's Preface – Key Debates in
  Educational Policy   vii
Foreword   xi
Christopher Winch
  The policy background in the United Kingdom   xiv

1 Teaching Thinking Skills   1
Stephen Johnson

  1. The argument   1
  2. Present interest in thinking skills   2
  3. Thinking as a skill   7
  4. General transferability   13
  5. Conceptual errors   20
  6. The direct teaching of thinking and the
     importance of content   25
  7. Thinking as mental processes   28
  8. Examples of general thinking skills   32
  9. The dangers   36
 10. Conclusion   42
     References   47

2 On Thinking Skills   51
Harvey Siegel

  1. Introduction   51
  2. Problems with thinking of thinking as a skill   54
  3. 'The myth of general transferability'   61
  4. The 'direct' teaching of thinking and
     content/subject matter knowledge   75

Contents

    5. Mental processes and general thinking skills   78
    6. The educational dangers of thinking of thinking in terms of skills   80
    7. Conclusion   82
       References   83
       Further reading   84

Afterword   **85**
Christopher Winch

    1. Skills   88
    2. Skills and transferability   96
    3. The question of efficacy   101
    4. What is thinking?   103
    5. Mental processes   104
    6. A summary of Johnson's claims   107
    7. Reasoning   109
    8. The role of philosophy   112
    9. Reason and argument   113
   10. Inductive arguments   120
   11. Concluding remarks   122
       References   123

Index   **125**

Series Editor's Preface – Key Debates in Educational Policy

IMPACT pamphlets were launched in 1999 as an initiative of the Philosophy of Education Society of Great Britain. Their aim was to bring philosophical perspectives to bear on UK education policy, and they have been written by leading general philosophers or philosophers of education. At the time of writing, 18 have been published.

They deal with a variety of issues relating to policy within the field of education. Some have focused on controversial aspects of current government policy such as those by Andrew Davis on assessment, Harry Brighouse on disparities in secondary education, Mary Warnock on changes in provision for pupils with special educational needs and Colin Richards on school inspection. Others, such as those by Michael Luntley on performance related pay and by Christopher Winch on vocational education and training, have been critical of new policy initiatives. Yet others have been concerned with the organization and content of the school curriculum. These have included pamphlets by Kevin Williams on the teaching of foreign languages, Steve Bramall and John White on Curriculum 2000, David Archard on sex education, Stephen Johnson on thinking skills, Graham Haydon on personal, social and health education, and John Gingell on the visual arts.

The launch of each pamphlet has been accompanied by a symposium for policy makers and others at which issues raised in the pamphlets have been further explored. These have been attended by government ministers, opposition spokespersons, other MPs, representatives from the Qualifications and Curriculum Authority, employers organizations, trades unions and teachers' professional organizations as well as members of think tanks, academics and journalists.

Some of the original pamphlets have made a lasting impression on the world of education policy and have, in addition, sparked debates in both the policy and academic worlds. They have revealed a hunger for dealing with certain topics in a philosophically oriented way because it has been felt that the original pamphlet initiated a debate in a mode of thinking about educational issues that needs and deserves to be taken a lot further. The Key Debates in Educational Policy series aims to take some of these debates further by selecting from those original Impact pamphlets whose influence continues to be keenly felt and either reproducing or expanding them to take account of the most recent developments in the area with which they deal. In addition, each of the original pamphlets receives a lengthy reply by a distinguished figure in the area who takes issue with the main arguments of the original pamphlet. Each of the Key Debates volumes also contains a substantial foreword and/or afterword by an academic with strong interests in the area under discussion, which gives the context and provides extensive commentary on the questions under discussion and the arguments of the original author and his/her respondent.

There are a number of reasons for doing this. Philosophical techniques applied to policy issues can be very powerful tools for clarifying questions and developing arguments based on ethical, aesthetic, political and epistemological positions. Philosophical argumentation is, however, by its nature, controversial and contested. There is rarely, if ever, one side to a philosophical question. The fact that the Impact pamphlets have often aroused lively debate and controversy is testament to this. There has been a desire for a more rounded version of the debate to be presented in a format accessible to those who do not have a formal philosophical background but who find philosophical argumentation about educational issues to be useful in developing their own ideas. This series aims to cater for this audience while also presenting rigorous argumentation that can also appeal to a more specialist audience.

It is hoped that each volume in this series will provide an introduction and set the scene to each topic and give the readership a splendid example of philosophical argumentation concerning a complex and important educational issue.

Foreword
Christopher Winch

This volume is about one of the most important educational issues that has been debated for many years on either side of the Atlantic. Both authors have made important contributions to the debate about thinking skills. Stephen Johnson's work is best known through his Impact pamphlet 'Teaching Thinking Skills', published by the Philosophy of Education Society of Great Britain in 2000, as well as various articles on the issue. Harvey Siegel has a long record of advocacy for the teaching of thinking skills in both books and articles and is especially well-known in the USA and Canada. They are both among the most distinguished contemporary contributors to this debate and it is a great opportunity for the interested public to be able to appreciate arguments of the highest quality on both sides of the debate.

One of the main questions that this volume is concerned with is the existence or otherwise of thinking skills. Whether or not they exist, the issues that they raise are considered to be very important, both by their proponents and their opponents. I will try and explain why. The proposed teaching of thinking skills (on the assumption that there are such things), whether it be in schools, colleges or universities, is thought to be important for two reasons relevant to education. The first is to do with the *aims* of education: to be able to think ably is thought to be a valued attribute of an educated person and one that the education system should strive to develop. I do not think that either of our contributors would dissent from this view. The second is to do with *pedagogic efficacy*, or the claim that the teaching of thinking skills is an efficient way of promoting learning and understanding of a wide range of subjects. There is undoubtedly more dispute over the contention that such skills can be taught, or, more controversially, over whether they can be taught in such a way that they can subsequently be applied to a range of subject matters. More radically, it is questioned whether such *general* or *transferable* skills actually exist. It is on these latter two issues, and especially on the last issue that the debate in this volume is largely centred.

To take the issue of educational aims first: it is often thought that, in a democratic society, where the public is reasonably well-informed about political matters and individuals are expected to be able to chart their own courses in life, the ability to think about all kinds of concerns through in an independent way is an essential attribute and one to be cultivated, at least indirectly, if not directly, within the education system. It does not follow directly from such a claim that general or transferable thinking skills are a prerequisite, but it at least gives some grounds for supposing this to be the case. The reason would be that in the case of public affairs it is necessary for citizens to make informed decisions about matters pertaining to the welfare of their society about which they do not necessarily possess specialist knowledge. They will either have to acquire specialist knowledge about such matters as the law, economics or physical geography for example or they will need to be able to understand and to make an intelligent appraisal of the arguments for and against positions adopted by lobby groups and public figures. The first possibility, we may take it, is highly unlikely even for highly educated people, as most will not have the time to do so, even if they have the inclination. Indeed, it is rare to find politicians with extensive or even any specialist knowledge of a subject relevant to the conduct of public affairs. In this type of case, to be more precise, they will need to equip themselves with powers of *critical reasoning*, which may be considered to be a subspecies of thinking skills.

In the case of conduct of one's own personal affairs and, more particularly in the matter of charting one's own course in life, the ability to think sensibly and intelligently about one's personal, financial, family and career affairs would seem to be highly desirable and something that one's education should make a significant contribution towards equipping one for. Even more than with the case of making informed judgements about public affairs, the need to be able to make informed judgements about one's personal affairs and those of individuals close to oneself would seem to be highly desirable and an expected outcome of any education in a modern society that would be worthy of the name 'education'. Even more than with the case of public affairs the need to be able to make informed judgements about matters of career, finance, relationships and one's own abilities in relation to a wide variety of circumstances and across a wide variety of subject matters seems to be highly desirable. And again, as with public affairs, the need to make informed judgements about matters concerning which one is not a specialist seems to be highly desirable, to put it mildly. The presumed desirability of teaching thinking skills that are general or transferable (or both) as a major aim of education, seems to be unanswerable.

The second issue, of pedagogic efficacy, is currently the focus of curriculum reform in England. The teaching of thinking skills, it is held, is valuable because it enables someone who has acquired those skills to become a more effective learner in more than one and, hopefully, many different subject matters. The ability to acquire and deploy thinking skills is, then, one important aspect of the widely proclaimed educational virtue of being able to *learn how to learn*, which in effect gives a student, or anyone engaged in learning, considerable autonomy in the sense that they should be able to acquire knowledge and understanding across a whole range of subject matters with relatively little pedagogic intervention. This claim of pedagogic efficacy is one where different kinds of claims are made, which are often difficult to evaluate. Perhaps the most difficult of these relates to the extent to which acquiring thinking skills enables one to dispense with learning and understanding the content of different subject areas. There is little doubt that suspicion of such claims is one of the factors motivating Johnson's critique of the teaching of thinking skills. On the other hand, it is possible to claim that the acquisition of thinking skills will enable one to learn how to learn more effectively without at the same time committing oneself to the view that there is a short cut to the 'hard way' of learning to master a subject. An alternative claim might be that the deployment of thinking skills in one's learning *together with* mastery of the subject is likely to produce a more thorough grasp of the subject than learning the subject matter without the benefit of thinking skills. It should be noted that there is nothing in Siegel's contribution that should lead us to suppose that he is inclined to take the former view.

The very way in which the debate on the usefulness or otherwise of thinking skills has been formulated itself causes difficulties which may be unnecessary complications of the issues involved. It is a major part of the purpose of the afterword to try and remove these complications where this is possible in order to try and make more precise the points of agreement and disagreement between Johnson and Siegel. The difficulties relate to both the terms 'thinking' and 'skill', both of which raise philosophical problems.

The policy background in the United Kingdom

The idea that there is an important place in the curriculum for the general development of mental powers is not new. In the United Kingdom, the study of classical languages such as Latin and Greek was advocated by some, not merely because of the knowledge that it gave to students of the civilizations that once used those languages, but because of the powers of logical thinking that their study was thought to confer on those who had mastered them. The decline of classics has thus arguably left a lacuna in the curriculum which the introduction of the teaching of thinking skills may be able to remedy.

Although the concepts of thinking skills and critical thinking have a long history of a place in the school curriculum in North America, their appearance in the United Kingdom in any significant form is more recent. They have appeared since 2000 as cross curricular threads in the National Curriculum in England and Wales and also in syllabuses as a formal subject 'Critical Thinking' at A level. In the National Curriculum they consist of *creative thinking, enquiry, evaluation, information processing* and *reasoning*. These headings are then subdivided, thus *reasoning* consists of the following abilities: giving reasons for opinions/actions, inferring, making deductions, making informed judgements/decisions and using precise language to reason. Although it is not stated that such abilities can be applied to different subject matters, one can infer that this is intended to be the case. If they were supposed to be different abilities in different contexts there would be no point in grouping them together as distinct, non-subject specific, abilities. There is little doubt that Johnson would object to these skills and their components in their entirety and would argue that none of them make sense without a specification of the subject matter to which they apply. For him, a non-subject specific, general, or transferable set of thinking skills or thinking abilities makes no sense and the search for one is in vain. This aspect of the National Curriculum would, therefore, on this view, be better if it did not exist.

However, the fact that it does exist is a testimony to the great faith that many, including governments, have in the existence of general and/or transferable thinking skills, in the possibility of teaching them and in their efficacy in promoting learning and understanding. This faith appears to be of quite a strong form, that any thinking skill acquired in one subject can be applied in another, given a certain threshold of knowledge in each subject. So Johnson's position and that set out in the National Curriculum seem to be diametrically opposed to each other. The national curriculum documentation recognizes that teachers will need guidance in teaching these thinking skills within their own subjects and gives explicit guidance as to how this is to be done in the form of brief case studies about particular subjects.

The stage is thus set for an assessment of whether such an approach is worthwhile and, more generally, whether thinking skills merit a place on the curriculum. Harvey Siegel adopts a position markedly more supportive of the general thrust of thinking skills programmes than does Johnson, although, as will be evident to the reader, there are important points of similarity between the two. How serious the differences are and whether or not they are reconcilable is a question that the reader will probably wish to ponder. In addition, the terms of the debate raise a number of issues, not just for those concerned with thinking skills *per se* but more broadly for those concerned with the role of thinking in professional and vocational activities and with the extent to which abilities are broad or narrow, transferable or non-transferable. I address some of these broader concerns, as well as taking up specific issues from this debate in a lengthy afterword to this exchange. The reader is advised to read the volume in sequence, making use of the afterword if he or she wishes to pursue some of the issues raised in greater depth.

Teaching Thinking Skills

Stephen Johnson

Chapter Outline

1. The argument — 1
2. Present interest in thinking skills — 2
3. Thinking as a skill — 7
4. General transferability — 13
5. Conceptual errors — 20
6. The direct teaching of thinking and the importance of content — 25
7. Thinking as mental processes — 28
8. Examples of general thinking skills — 32
9. The dangers — 36
10. Conclusion — 42
    References — 47

1. The argument

The Government in Britain is taking a keen interest in the development of thinking skills. An early indication of and impetus to this interest was the Government's commissioning of the *From Thinking Skills to Thinking Classrooms* report. The influence of this report has been such that thinking skill are now part of the National Curriculum and Critical Thinking Skills is a popular Advanced Level subject.

However, treating thinking as a skill is based on serious and educationally damaging misconceptions:

1. The appeal of thinking skills rests largely on the view that they are generally transferable. This view is mistaken.
2. The myth of general transferability rests upon a number of fallacies and conceptual errors.
3. The direct approach to teaching thinking can lead to knowledge playing a subsidiary role and even being seen as an impediment.
4. 'Mental processes' are dubious entities and access to them is highly problematic. They support the myth of general transferability and encourage a checklist approach to thinking.
5. Suggested examples of general thinking skills do not stand up to examination.
6. Thinking skills present dangers: the disparagement of knowledge, the impersonalizing and neutralizing of thought, the neglect of truth, and the computerization of thought.

The inclusion of thinking skills in the National Curriculum is thus hasty and ill-considered. It is also inconsistent with a curriculum that treats subjects as self-contained units. A thorough grounding in curriculum areas of knowledge is therefore recommended, together with developing certain habits of mind.

2. Present interest in thinking skills

Recently the British Government has taken a direct interest in the teaching of thinking skills.

'The Government regard thinking as a key part of the national curriculum,' stated the Department for Education and Employment (Hansard, 1 July 1999). 'Pupils to learn how to think', announced

Teaching Thinking Skills

The Guardian (6 January 2000). Well this seems as surprising as a sermon against sin. Who would not want children to be taught how to think? However, when *The Guardian* goes on to say that 'All pupils are to be taught thinking skills,' the project begins to raise questions. When general thinking skills are being proposed, we have moved from truism to controversy.

Many educationalists, however, believe that there are general thinking skills. Such skills are thought to be non-subject specific and generally transferable. I address two main questions: are objections to general thinking skills sufficiently powerful to cast serious doubt on their educational value and even on their existence? Are there educational dangers in characterizing thinking in terms of such skills?

No doubt many earlier generations of teachers wanted their pupils to become better at thinking, but they did not employ the notion of general thinking skills. Why then is this notion so much in vogue at present? First, skills are viewed as having a simplicity and objectivity which renders them readily identifiable and easily broken down into component sub-skills. Skills seem to answer the many demands made on education: that teaching must be more efficient and effective; that students must be assessed in a more fine-grained way; that the educational emphasis must be placed on the quantifiable, the instrumental and the vocationally useful. Secondly, there is currently the expectation that all phases of education will equip students with general transferable skills, and general thinking skills are high on this particular agenda. Consequently, in teaching there is pressure to move from the transmission of knowledge to the teaching of supposed intellectual skills such as thinking.

The UK Government's Standards Site dates the huge growth of interest in the teaching of thinking skills from the publication in 1999 of a Department for Education and Skills (DfEE) report by Dr Carol McGuinness: *From Thinking Skills to Thinking*

4 Teaching Thinking Skills

Classrooms: a review and evaluation of approaches for developing pupils' thinking (hereafter the McGuinness Report):

> Since the review by Carol McGuinness in 1999 and the explicit inclusion of thinking skills in the National Curriculum, interest in the teaching of thinking skills has burgeoned in the UK. (DfES, 2008)

The Schools Standards Minister welcomed the McGuinness Report as 'this excellent report' and claimed that it had shown that for pupils to think they must be 'taught explicitly' how to do it and that 'emphasising the quality of thinking processes and thinking skills is a means of raising standards.'

The Government speedily acted on this Report. Within a few months, the Secretary of State for Education announced that all children were to be taught thinking skills. Thinking skills were included in the National Curriculum. Materials on thinking skills were developed for the National Key Stage 3 Strategy. This was followed by thinking skills initiatives such as *Teaching and Learning in the Foundation Subjects* (DfES, 2004b) and *Leading in Learning* (DfES, 2005). Furthermore, thinking skills are now an important part of the Primary National Strategy (DfES, 2004a), and the influence of the McGuinness Report can be seen in the development of a database of thinking skills resources for primary schools on the Government's Standards Site (DfES, 2008). Rarely, if ever, has so concise a report had so considerable an influence on educational policy. This tide of enthusiasm for thinking skills has also been felt in the post-statutory sector where it has raised Critical Thinking Skills to a very popular Advanced Level examination subject (at AS and, more recently, at A2 level).

i. The McGuinness Report

The author of the report is the former director of the Activating Children's Thinking Skills project funded by the Northern Ireland Council for Curriculum, Examination and Assessment. As this report continues to provide the Government with its main academic authority on the theoretical foundation for teaching thinking skills, I use it as a platform for my discussion. I shall, therefore, be considering some of the report's key conclusions: that thinking is best conceived of as a skill; that thinking skills should be made explicit; that students must be explicitly and directly taught thinking skills; that transfer is crucially important; that students should make explicit, and reflect upon, their own thought processes and cognitive strategies (a metacognitive approach); and that 'considerable evaluation work remains to be done' (McGuinness Report, p. 1).

McGuinness highlights the need for thinking skills programmes to have a 'strong theoretical underpinning' (p. 1). I would suggest that part of the evaluation work remaining to be done is an enquiry into the theoretical underpinning of the McGuinness Report itself. This includes: construing thinking as a skill, the conviction that thinking is a matter of processing information, and belief in general thinking skills, such as analysing and hypothesizing.

McGuinness outlines three main approaches to teaching thinking: the general, the subject-specific and the infusion approach. The *general* approach maintains, according to McGuinness, that 'cognitive development is driven by a general central processor and that intervention at this level will have widespread effects across many thinking domains' (p. 7). All programmes adopting this approach aim to develop general information processing abilities, but whereas some are context-free, employing specially designed materials (e.g., Somerset Thinking Skills Course, Blagg et al., 1988; Mentis and Dunn-Bernstein, M., 2008)), others target general cognitive development from within particular subject areas (e.g., Cognitive Acceleration through Science Education (CASE), see Shayer and Adey, 2002). The *subject-specific* approach aims to enhance thinking within domain-specific contexts; an example of this is the *Thinking through History* project (Fisher, 2002), which also features general problem-solving and emphasizes metacognition.

Finally, we have the approach personally favoured by McGuinness, the *infusion* method. It is generic in character, but seeks to embed thinking skills within curricular areas by utilizing opportunities for developing general thinking skills within curriculum subjects.

As my main concern is with general thinking skills, it would seem that the *general* approach is most obviously germane. The *infusion* method, however, is also highly relevant here, as it appears to use subject content merely as convenient hooks on which to hang general thinking skills. For, as McGuinness puts it, 'this approach does have a generic character, it seeks to embed thinking skills . . . and exploit naturally occurring opportunities for developing thinking within the ordinary curriculum' (p. 19). So, with the infusion approach, contexts within the curriculum are identified where general thinking skills can be developed. As for the aptness of the term 'infusion', McGuinness states that, according to the dictionary, 'to infuse' means to 'introduce into one thing a second which gives it extra life, vigour and a new significance' (p. 19). It would appear from this that thinking skills are not seen as integral to a subject, but are to be introduced 'from the outside'. These observations also hold for the subject-specific approaches, where the main focus is also general thinking skills.

McGuinness's classification has been reorganized by the British Government's Standards Site database. Here the thinking skills programmes are grouped in the following three categories: Cognitive Intervention (e.g., Feuerstein's and other psychological theories), Brain-based Approaches (e.g., de Bono) and Philosophical Approaches (e.g., Lipman). There is considerable overlap between these and '[t]here are clear similarities in each of the categories' (DfES, 2008, p. 3).

In whatever way the different programmes are categorized the dominant paradigm is that of information processing (see McGuinness Report, p. 4), with an emphasis on learners reflecting on, and articulating, their cognitive strategies. The primacy of process, rather than content, is stressed, as is the importance attached to experts making their mental processes explicit. Furthermore, all the programmes try to teach certain general thinking skills. These shared aspects are consistent with the view that thinking is a skill, a proposition I now examine.

3. Thinking as a skill

Treating thinking as a skill can create educational dangers.

There is no doubt the McGuinness Report raises many important issues. The report says that one of its main purposes is to analyse what is currently understood by the term 'thinking skills' (p. 1). It is acknowledged that some people have misgivings about the term 'skill' being applied to thinking, but the report insists that seeing thinking as a skill has 'both theoretical and instructional force' (p. 4). McGuinness believes that 'much of what we know about skill learning can be usefully applied to developing thinking' (p. 5).

But it is an important question whether thinking is misconceived as a skill and an important further question whether if it is, this misconception is innocuous or pernicious – might it, for instance, lead to inappropriate pedagogy?

Robert Fisher's book, *Teaching Children to Think*, carries an epigraph from Ryle: 'All lessons are lessons in thinking.' Fisher neglects, however, to point out that Ryle thought that teaching thinking skills would be plainly 'ridiculous' (1979, p. 66). Fisher continues: 'We teach children many skills, physical skills, social skills, expressive skills, linguistic and mathematical skills, why not thinking skills?' (1990, p. x). Fisher's question is apparently rhetorical for it is never referred to again, much less addressed. One possible response to the question, 'Why not teach thinking skills?' would be to pose a series of related questions: Why not teach wisdom skills? Why not teach originality skills? Why not teach good judgement skills? Why not teach accuracy skills or truth-seeking skills?

Mention of 'accuracy' and 'truth-seeking' bring to mind a danger in seeing thinking as a skill. For with a skill, the failure to exhibit it does not in itself count against its possession. It would be wrong to conclude that X could not ride a bicycle simply because X fails to take the opportunity to ride a bicycle, for one can be said to possess a skill that, once acquired, one does not choose to exercise – though it is true that some skills may atrophy if not used. This lack of connection between possession and performance in the case of skills contrasts with personal qualities, virtues and aspects of character, for to possess a virtue, for example, is to be disposed to act in a certain way. This is because there is a close relationship between possessing aspects of character and exercising them. So failure to exercise a virtue (given the opportunity) on any particular occasion will count against, though not completely refute, the claim that one has that virtue. I am not here concerned with the question of verification or behavioural evidence, but with the logical connection between possessing a characteristic and exercising it. My point may be illustrated by considering two claims: (a) I have the skill of swimming but, despite opportunities, I've chosen not to exercise it for 30 years; and (b) I have the virtue of kindness but, despite opportunities, I've chosen not to exercise it for 30 years.

This lack of entailment between possession and performance is connected with the notion that skills are peripheral to the personality. By calling thinking a skill we may lose sight of the dispositional side of thinking, overlooking that thinking is continuous with our humanity and constitutive of it. That some personal qualities and capacities are integral to the personality is related to questions of commitment to truth and the relationship between knowledge, virtue and education.

There are other ways of differentiating between skills, virtues and knowledge. One emerges from the question: if skills are associated with performing an action, how are we to pick out the range of verbs that are appropriate to this sort of action? I would propose that a necessary, though not a sufficient, condition of something being a skill is that it must make good linguistic sense to tell someone to do it. This imperative-based test would exclude from being skills such educationally crucial concepts as 'knowledge', 'belief', 'understanding' and 'appreciation'.

An apparent difficulty for this argument is presented by the virtues and such imperative mood verb phrases as 'be honest,' or 'be kind.' In such cases, however, it is not an action that is being named, therefore no skill is indicated; the imperative here indicates the manner in which some action should be performed. I would also suggest that in many cases such imperatives are an elliptical way of giving an instruction to act in a particular way. If a lawyer advises you to 'Be honest,' he may well mean 'Tell the truth.' Similarly, 'Be kind', might mean 'Give him some money.'

Scheffler proposes another method of differentiating. His test is not based on the imperative, but on the interrogative. In answers to the question 'What are you doing?' it makes good sense to reply, 'I am swimming,' or 'I am typing,' but not 'I am knowing', or 'I am believing'. Scheffler concludes from this that 'As in the case of understanding and appreciation . . . knowing does not seem to fit performance, activity or skill categories at all' (1965, p. 27). I believe that Scheffler's approach could also be used to differentiate between virtues and skills, though Scheffler himself does not use it in this way. For instance, if in reply to the question 'What are you doing?' someone replied 'I am being honest' or 'I am being kind,' then, although they may be telling the truth, there is a sense in which they are not telling you what they are doing.

Despite the difficulties, McGuinness insists on treating thinking as a skill. The reasons given for this reveal much about the conception of thinking held by those who advocate teaching thinking. And as this is the conception that is enshrined in the National Curriculum, it is important to examine these reasons.

10 Teaching Thinking Skills

(a) 'it places thinking firmly on the side of 'knowing-how' rather than 'knowing that' (p. 4)

But this distinction between know-how and know-that can be educationally unhelpful. It may, for instance, divorce beliefs from actions, and drive a wedge between mental processes, which are taken to be active, and knowledge, which is taken to be inert. We will encounter this passivity-grounded and reductive view of propositional knowledge later for it is consistent with the information-processing model of the brain, which is such a dominant paradigm in many thinking skills programmes. In contrast to this inert view, the standard analysis of propositional knowledge is that such knowledge requires a belief and hence understanding, the belief being based upon a rationale the force of which is appreciated by the knower.

Placing 'thinking firmly on the side of know-how' also seems inappropriate in the case of thinking when it is remembered that to have mastered a skill usually means to be able to exercise it without thinking. Barrow considers skill to be only 'minimally involved with understanding' (1987, pp. 190–191). Scheffler takes the same line, for after stating that '*knowing how to* represents the possession of a skill' (1965, p. 92, original italics), he adds that *knowing how* is applicable in cases 'where repeated trial, or practice, is thought relevant to performance and where it is carried out under minimal conditions of understanding' (p. 93). Both Barrow and Scheffler are saying you can have a skill without understanding the theories that may underpin it; one can ride a bicycle, for example, without understanding theories which explain why one does not fall off. The fact that the exercise of a skill does not necessarily require thought is illustrated by Thomas Hardy's lines in *The Dynasts*:

> Like a knitter drowsed,
> Whose fingers play in skilled unmindfulness (Hardy, 1931, pt.i).

In other words, in some cases one may exercise a skill without concentrating on, or perhaps even being consciously aware of, what one is doing.

(b) It focuses attention on 'being explicit about components of the skill' (p. 5)

It is often believed that skills can be analysed into sub-skills, or components, and that these components can be sequentially and hierarchically organized. This would appear inappropriate in the case of thinking and may have a baleful influence if it leads to unsuitable approaches to encouraging intelligent thinking: 'Come young master Einstein, enough of these flashes of insight, think things through stage by stage.'

Perhaps the most telling argument against this reductive view of skills is that it does not even apply to many model cases of skill, such as crafts and sports, let alone those areas that are far more problematic as far as skill-talk is concerned. The footballer David Beckham doesn't go through a checklist covering positioning of feet, body angle, follow-through and the like in order to centre the ball. If he did, he wouldn't be David Beckham. Similarly physical and practical skills of any complexity cannot be adequately taught by breaking each skill down into components: teaching 'parts' is no guarantee that the learner acquires the whole. Although it is possible to analyse a physical skill into more basic components, the whole is usually greater than the sum of these components. Consequently, it is difficult to imagine how someone could be taught to ride a bicycle, for instance, by breaking the skill of cycling down into components, whatever they might be, and then learning each component separately.

Although my central argument is that a reductionist approach to teaching skills is likely to be unsuccessful in many important cases, because mastery of the so-called 'sub-skills' still leaves the learner well short of mastering the whole, as a rider to this argument I also wish to attack the view often held by these reductionists that teaching rules and principles is essential. Learning principles that describe the physics of cycling, for example, need not help us to learn how to ride a bicycle. One could give a lengthy, technical description of the rules that a cyclist could be said to be observing, but the cyclist could not consciously apply these rules. She could not, for instance, under normal circumstances, calculate the ratio of unbalance over the square of her speed and then adjust the curvature of her path in proportion to it; cyclists don't have the time or, in most cases, the mathematical ability.

Getting students to become conscious of underlying rules or principles may even distract from the execution of a skill. Indeed, in many cases focusing attention on the details will paralyse a performer – in golf this is known as 'paralysis by analysis'. It is like the centipede immobilized by the question, 'pray, which leg goes after which?' Or consider the pianist who ruins her performance by thinking of what she is doing with her fingers.

(c) It stresses 'learning by observing and modelling' (p. 5)

While observing and modelling might be useful ways of trying to emulate carpenters or gardeners, this won't work with thinkers; thoughts, unlike a carpenter's work at the lathe, are private. We cannot observe a thinker's thinking skills! But it isn't just a matter of privacy; it is also the failure of models to capture the reality of our thoughts. Although expert carpenters may go through the same stages in making the same type of article – such that a standard flow chart of the construction process could be produced – it is unlikely that the thoughts of expert thinkers will fit a common model, even if they reach the same conclusion. For instance, there is no mental process of remembering common to all acts of memory. Norman Malcolm gives the example of remembering putting one's keys in the kitchen drawer – one may remember in several ways: 1. Mentally retrace steps and get a mental image of putting the keys in the drawer; 2. Nothing occurs to you, ask yourself and exclaim 'the kitchen drawer'; 3. Asked while deep in conversation, you point to the drawer; 4. Writing a letter you walk to the drawer and take out the keys while composing the next sentence; 5. Without hesitation you answer directly. There would not appear to be any uniform process of memory.

(d) It points out 'the importance of practice' (p. 5)

de Bono also has no doubt that thinking 'is a skill that can be improved by practice' (1978, p. 45). This is the 'training of mental muscles' approach we will encounter again when we come to the influence of faculty psychology. de Bono provides a good example of this when he recommends 'thinking about simple things where you get answers. In that way you will build up your skills in thinking' (1996, p. 253). But the arithmetical circuit-training of simple sums seems to prepare one only for simple sums.

Practice seems appropriate in the case of a skill where one can decide to exercise the skill and then monitor and control it with respect to a known end-product. This is less clearly the case in the area of the intellect, for one cannot choose to understand something – we can neither initiate nor control it. In addition, thinking will often not have a known end-product; it will often lead to more questions or deeper perplexity.

Another reason given by McGuinness for regarding thinking as a skill is that it underlines 'the importance of . . . transfer of learning' (p. 5). But a skill might have a severely restricted range of application. McGuinness must, therefore, have in mind general transferable skills. Indeed, if such 'skills' as thinking were not thought to have general transferability they would lose much of their educational attraction.

4. General transferability

Much of the educational appeal of thinking skills stems from a mistaken belief in their general transferability.

McGuinness says that 'maximising the transfer of learning beyond the context in which it was learned is at the heart of the matter' (p. 8). In many ways this is indeed the crux of the issue: are there domain independent thinking skills? Many believe that there are. Scriven, for example, speaks of Critical Thinking as 'a finite set of skills in using a finite set of tools' (1990, p. xi), skills that, he claims, 'can . . . be taught without the need for delving into vast subject matters' (p. x). Such skills offers the huge educational bonus of being able to, for example, solve problems in many or every domain without the chore of the detailed learning of specific content. Furthermore, not being tied to content would help these skills to avoid obsolescence, and being generally transferable would make these skills very useful in the workplace.

Yet in a minimal and trivial sense all skills are transferable in so far as all skills can be repeated in relevantly similar circumstances – this may be referred to as 'portability'. But are thinking skills especially transferable?

The idea of transfer itself is far more problematic than is generally recognized. Transfer depends not only on there being an appropriate similarity between contexts, but also on this similarity being perceived by the person transferring the skill.

Nelson Goodman, writing of the elusive nature of the notion of similarity, says: 'whether two actions are instances of the same behaviour depends upon how we take them' (1970, p. 22). In other words, judgements about the sameness of human performances require a 'theory' in the sense of being in need of some interpretation or explanation. Wittgenstein says that a student has been taught to understand when he can independently continue with a sequence or procedure, 'If he succeeds he exclaims: 'Now I can go on!' (1958, p. 59). Wittgenstein's point about being able to continue with a sequence or procedure requires the application of a particular rule. But, as Kripke explains, after, for example, the sequence 2, 4, 6, 8, . . . 'an indefinite number of rules . . . are compatible with any such finite initial segment', so he concludes that there is no such thing as 'the unique appropriate next number' (1993, p. 18). Any interpretation will need to include the beliefs and intentions of the agent, as well as the social settings. In some social settings, for example, the correct continuation of the sequence 2, 4, 6, 8, is 'who do we appreciate'! As Lave and Wenger have observed, activities and tasks 'do not exist in isolation; they are part of a broader system of relations in which they have meaning. These systems of relations arise out of and are reproduced and developed within social communities' (1991, p. 53). So, as Davis points out, what is to count as 'same again' 'usually cannot be gleaned from a consideration of the performance detached from its context and the meaning attached to it by the agent, and her community' (1996, p. 14). As may be appreciated from this, the difficulties these issues raise for the transfer of skills become particularly acute for skills claiming to enjoy general transferability to all, or most, contexts.

With respect to thinking skills, one aspect of the context will be the domain of knowledge in which one is operating. I am not, of course, arguing that domains of knowledge are hermetically sealed. Between domains there are complex connections and shared concepts. In opposing the general transferability of thinking skills one could simply observe that whether or not aesthetics and physics are well connected or barely connected domains, there is little evidence to suggest that studying classical ballet or Titian are sufficient or necessary or even useful in becoming a rocket scientist.

General transferable skills raise high expectations, but also create the sort of doubts expressed by many researchers. Perkins, for example, after examining a number of studies, observed that they provided no support for the existence of such skills; he concluded: 'It is easy to extend this list of negatives and "don't knows", but I have no firm positives to add' (1985, p. 348). Singley and Anderson also failed to discover any general transfer of cognitive skills and summarized their findings: 'Besides this spate of negative evidence, there has been no positive evidence of general transfer' (1989, p. 25). Later Singley writes that 'nearly a century of research in psychology has generated a depressing lack of evidence for the notion of general transfer' (1995, p. 69). Besides the difficulty of proving a negative, what sustains belief in these skills? Anderson offers an explanation: 'one reason why general transfer keeps rising from the grave is that it is such an attractive proposition for psychologists and educators alike' (1993, p. 25). Such skills are simply too good not to be true.

But what theories might underpin the idea of general transfer? I briefly examine three theories and consider the extent to which they might support general transferable thinking skills.

i. Faculty psychology

Faculty psychology is the theory that the mind is divided up into separate powers or faculties. Despite seemingly devastating criticism (see, for example, James (1890)), this theory has proved to be remarkably resilient. The theory loses every intellectual battle, but survives and, apart from dropping the word 'faculty', seems to escape scot-free.

One of the places to which this theory has escaped is the area of thinking skills. The exploded theory of faculty psychology underpins notions of general powers of the mind and the existence of general thinking skills such as observation, judgement, imagination and critical thinking. This leads to the view that someone can think critically, solve problems or be imaginative, regardless of context or situation.

The learning theory developed on the basis of faculty psychology was that of formal discipline. This theory maintains that faculties, such as imagination, reasoning or memory, are like mental muscles that can be built up by undertaking the appropriate tasks. Formal discipline is so called because it maintains that the *form* of studies, rather than their *content*, imparts mental training. Hence, in many thinking skills programmes any subject matter may be chosen as long as it exercises certain generic abilities. The City and Guilds Diploma of Vocational Education, for example, contains the 'general skill' of 'Making Decisions', and this, we are told, can be taught by using any content the teacher wishes (City and Guilds, 1991, p. 74).

The main fault with this theory is assuming that for each of a whole range of mentalistic verbs there exists a particular faculty, a particular part of a person's mind, which is exercised whenever a sentence involving the verb can be applied to that person. Yet surely the fact that I doubt (wonder, speculate, conjecture . . .), does not mean I am exercising my faculty of doubting (wondering, speculating, conjecturing . . .).

It is the theory of faculty psychology that helps to underpin notions of general powers of the mind and the existence of general thinking skills, such as, observation, judgement, imagination, critical thinking and creativity. This leads to the view that someone can think critically, solve problems or be imaginative *simpliciter*, regardless of context.

ii. Identical elements

According to this theory, in order for learned responses to be transferred there have to be identical elements between the two situations. This reveals a certain naiveté with regard to the notion of 'identity'. As I have indicated, even the less rigorous notion of 'similarity' can be elusive. The difficulties of stereotyping mathematical ability for example, on the basis of the similarity of operations, have been illustrated by Ruthven (1988).

If identical elements do occur in two learning situations it is maintained that transfer would be automatic. Of course, any failure to transfer could always elicit the response that identical elements could not have been involved, but on this basis the thesis could become trivial and of little or no educational relevance.

In the USA, a generation of curriculum planners adopted this approach. On this model there are three steps in constructing a curriculum: (1) divide life into major activities, (2) analyse these activities into specific skills, (3) make these skills your behavioural objectives (see Bobbitt, 1926, p. 9).

This approach to finding the common skills needed to live a socially and economically useful life bears a striking resemblance to the methods used in Britain to establish skills designated as 'basic' or 'core'. Examples of such skills are: 'Find out facts about things that have gone wrong,' 'Decide when action is required,' 'Decide how to make the best of an awkward situation,' and 'Manipulate objects or materials' (MSC, 1984, p. 37), 'making decisions' and 'weighing up pros and cons' (McGuinness Report, p. 5). But of course there is no common skill involved in, for example, finding out how a marriage has gone wrong, how an engine has gone wrong, or how a philosophical argument has gone wrong.

iii. Information processing

The final theory of learning transfer emanates from cognitive psychology. This theory proposes that the brain is an information processor, and that there are three sets of components: input, output and control. It is argued that it is the control strategy or general plan that is important in transfer. This approach is prominent in the McGuinness Report and in a number of educational programmes that aim to teach general thinking skills, for example, Instrumental Enrichment (Feuerstein et al., 1980).

Goal-setting is often considered to be a good example of this approach, and McGuinness has 'setting up goals and sub goals' as a thinking skill (p. 5). But what general plan could control all goal-setting? In the absence of guidance we could speculate: goals should be as clear as possible; never choose goals that are impossible except where pursuing the impossible itself is a goal; a goal is impossible if the means are impossible; before selecting goals decide on your priorities; select goals which, if achieved, would best satisfy your priorities. Such principles are, of course, in the main, vacuous. But such vacuity is frequently encountered in the area of thinking skills. Consider, for instance, the occupational information site *onetcenter*. Here we find problem solving skills defined as 'developed capacities used to solve novel, ill-defined problems in real-world settings'. Problem solving skills are then said to involve 'identifying complex problems and reviewing related information to develop and evaluate options and implement solutions' (onetcenter, 2008). Employers would surely be deluding themselves if they believed that such empty truisms could help in selecting, for instance, the best chemical engineer, chef or teacher. This highlights a pervasive and intractable problem for all general thinking skills and for the information-processing model of transfer in particular: as the generality of the principles increases, their usefulness and effectiveness decrease.

This approach raises the question of what in turn controls the control strategy and thus opens up the prospect of infinite regress. As Ryle (1949, p. 31) notes, if we had to plan what to think before thinking it we would never think at all, because this planning would itself need to be thought about, which would need planning, which would itself need . . . and so on.

Finally, this theory raises a question concerning the status of these strategies. Are they created techniques or heuristics like, for instance, a mnemonic, or are they processes that go on in the brain? Sternberg writes that the 'status of these classification schemes is not entirely clear at the present time' (1982, p. 7). However, in his own work Sternberg claims to have discovered a number of general processes that are involved in thinking. But I would contend that Sternberg did not so much discover these processes as postulate them on the basis of what he thought was involved in solving a problem. The danger is that of assuming that processes are going on in us by reading back from a product of some sort to the idea that certain mental processes must have occurred – an example of faulty thinking if ever there was one.

5. Conceptual errors

The myth of the general transferability of thinking skills may rest upon certain fallacies.

Philosophers have long realized that common linguistic usage may lead us into the ontological error of assuming the existence of non-existent entities or properties, or at least of ascribing to them an inaccurate ontological status. Anselm of Canterbury, for example, observed that 'many things are said to *be* something or other according to the form of the spoken expression, which in fact are *not* anything: we just speak about them as we do really existing things' (cited in Henry, 1984. p. 12). I now concentrate on four, often interconnected, conceptual errors prevalent in discussions about general thinking skills.

i. Reification

Reification is the act of wrongly treating X as if it were a *thing*. There might, however, be nothing wrong with treating lots of things as things, but it is important to treat them as the right sorts of things. One example of this error that is germane to our present inquiry is that, although we can refer to 'thinking', there is no such thing as 'thinking' *tout court*. This is because 'think' takes an indirect object.

Another example of reification of particular relevance here is moving from the properly adverbial or adjectival to the improperly substantive. It is often assumed that if X can do Y skilfully, there must be a skill of Y-ing and that X has it. For example, because it is meaningful to talk of someone who thinks well as being a skilful thinker, we are tempted to believe that there is a 'skill' to be identified, isolated and trained for. Thus there is in effect a jump from talk of performing an action well or successfully to the existence of some specific, discrete skill or skills possessed by and exercised by the performer, the very name of which is given, or at least suggested, in the description of the successful performance. This can have the unfortunate consequence of classing as skills activities and attributes that are ill suited to such a description. This error may be illustrated by de Bono's claim: 'Manifestly thinking is a skill in as much as thinking can be performed skilfully' (de Bono, 1978, p. 45).

ii. Essentialism

Essentialists in this area believe that just as acid has the power to turn litmus red or a magnet has the power to attract iron filings because of some underlying structure, so the ability to solve problems or to think critically is explicable in terms of underlying structures of the mind or brain. Hence, Norris writes:

> to say that someone has critical thinking ability is to make a claim about a mental power which that person possesses. Mental powers, in turn, arise from mental structures and processes in the same way that physical powers (magnetism is an example) arise from internal structures and processes of physical objects (1990, p. 68).

But transferring this idea from inorganic substances to human intellectual abilities can have unfortunate results. It may lead to motivation, beliefs, desires and context being ignored. Furthermore, general labels such as 'problem-solving' or 'critical thinking' gain a spurious unity and precision. Finally, this idea makes it difficult to explain how someone with the mental power of critical thinking could ever fail to think critically, in the same way as it would be difficult to explain why a magnet failed to attract iron filings or why an acid didn't turn litmus red.

iii. Naming fallacy

This fallacy is committed by supposing the existence of a general skill or ability X, from the existence of a general label or category, X. In other words, because we have a general name which can be correctly applied to a range of activities, then it is assumed that there must be a general skill corresponding to that general name. For instance, because there is the general label of, say, 'evaluating' then there must be a general skill of evaluating.

I believe this fallacy may play a role in some defences of general thinking skills (see Siegel, 1990, pp. 76–77 and Bailin and Siegel, 2003, p. 184). Siegel says that a conception of thinking 'must be possible, on pain of inability to identify all specific acts as acts of thinking'. Ryle, however, argues that some concepts, such as 'working' and 'thinking', are polymorphous, in that there need be nothing in common between different examples of thinking. He writes:

> There is no general answer to the question 'What does thinking consist of?' There are hosts of widely different sorts of toilings and idlings, engaging in any one of which is thinking. Yet there need be nothing going on in one of them, such that something else of the same species or genus must be going on in another of them. (cited by Urmson, 1970, p. 250)

Wittgenstein uses a different approach to show that there need be nothing in common between all examples of a concept such as thinking. In his notion of family resemblance he states that, in the case of games, for example, 'you will not find something common to all, but similarities, relationships' (1958, p. 31); instead of a common feature running through all instances of a concept, there is a network of overlapping similarities. Such a concept is best illustrated by giving a range of examples rather than looking for general features.

I assume that if Ryle or Wittgenstein is right then those arguing for general thinking skills on the basis that all examples of thinking have common features would have a problem.

However, even if we put these arguments to one side, it does not follow that being able to define 'thinking' entitles us to suppose the existence of general skills of thinking. The proper use of the concept 'thinking' will take note of the fact that we can only think about *something*; there must be some object of thought. Consider as an analogy the concept 'wanting': there are criteria for the proper use of the concept 'wanting', one of which is that the verb 'want' cannot be used properly unless something is wanted, but this does not mean that everything that wants, wants the same thing.

Siegel's argument for general thinking skills seems to move from the characterization of a concept which need not entail existence (consider, for example, fairies, or hobgoblins) to the existence of a general activity which, even if it is a verb that applies to human beings, may not be possible (e.g., levitating or becoming invisible) and thence to the existence of certain skills. But general human activities do not necessarily involve skills (grieving or believing, for example).

So because we can recognize specific acts as acts of 'judging', or 'being accurate', it does not follow that there are corresponding general skills, such that we could coherently claim to be able to teach a person judging skills or accuracy skills *simpliciter*.

An analogy capturing the complexity and polymorphous nature of 'thinking' would be 'working', but who could claim to teach the general skills of working? Siegel supports his argument with an analogy between cycling and thinking, pointing out that we can teach people general skills of cycling (1990, p. 77). This, however, is not very convincing, partly for the reasons given earlier for not regarding thinking as a skill, and partly because cycling is, in fact, a very specific activity rather than a general one, with an obvious and limited set of standards and criteria of effectiveness. Moreover, bicycles seem much more alike than, for instance, areas of critical thought such as chemistry and aesthetics.

In fact, the most Siegel could claim from his analogy would be a degree of transferability, but only in the trivial sense that all skills and abilities are transferable in that they are repeatable in relevantly similar circumstances. Therefore, if repeatability were a criterion for generality, then all skills and abilities would be general, as repeatability is the criterion for possessing any skill or ability.

The analogy would be somewhat stronger if Siegel were saying that if one can ride a bicycle one has the skills necessary for riding a horse, a surf-board and a punch, as riding is a general activity of which cycling is but one specific example. Unfortunately for Siegel, however, this strengthening of the analogy would be purchased at the cost of increased implausibility.

iv. Generalizing fallacy

This error consists in putting a task competence under the heading of a wider, perhaps an extremely wide, task descriptor and assuming that if a person has mastered the task competence then, *ipso facto*, she can do whatever falls under the wider descriptor. So, if a person has mastered a task competence X, say that of knowing how to use a tin opener, and X falls under a broader and more general heading Y, say of using a device for opening things or even using a tool, then the person can do whatever falls under Y, that is, the person can use any device that opens things or even can use all tools. This fallacy involves at least two errors. First, there is the naming fallacy, which, as we have seen, assumes that because a general category of activities can be named then there exists a corresponding inclusive skill. Secondly, it is assumed that to master one or a few skills that fall within this general category means that one simply has the general skill and all it encompasses. Such reasoning, if not corrected, can be seen to justify a move from the original task competence into situations that are relevantly, even extravagantly, dissimilar. This fallacious move helps account for the crucial role 'skills' play in youth training and pre-vocational education; for training in such skills would fit trainees for an incredibly wide range of tasks and occupations. The Core Skills Programme of the Youth Training Scheme (MSC, 1984) provides some examples: 'Decision making, e.g., decide which category something belongs to.' Also, see the 'general skill,' of 'decision making' cited on page 17 above (City and Guilds, 1991). A more recent example is the present so-called Key Skill of 'working with others' (Qualifications and Curriculum Authority, 2008a).

All three theories of transfer may encourage people to accept as correct the generalizing fallacy. Faculty psychology proposes that because a number of activities fall under one broad faculty heading, for example 'creativity', then there is some transfer between creativity on a football pitch and creativity in the physics laboratory. The identical elements theory has a proclivity to classify tasks on the basis of a very wide common element. In practice this has led to absurd claims such as those who can use kitchen knives have acquired the wider general transferable skill of 'cutting with one blade' (FEU, 1982, p. 72). Beware of brain surgeons who trained as lumberjacks! Finally, the theory that relies on the existence of general strategies proposes that there is such a thing as, for example, problem-solving *simpliciter* (see Qualifications and Curriculum Authority, 2008a). Thus there could appear to be some transfer between finding what is wrong with an inoperative washing machine and spotting the flaw in an invalid syllogism. Such strategies and processes are thought, once again, to be too good not to be true, as they seem to promise the educational holy grail of generalizability.

Moving on from the general transferability of thinking skills, let us now consider the proposal that thinking skills should be taught directly.

6. The direct teaching of thinking and the importance of content

In pursuit of the direct teaching of thinking, knowledge is viewed not only as subsidiary but as an actual impediment.

Many supporters of thinking skills believe that 'If students are to become better thinkers . . . then they *must* be taught explicitly how to do it. We cannot suppose that they will spontaneously learn how to think from teaching science or mathematics or history' (McGuinness Report, p. 4, my italics). One wonders how good, or even competent, thinkers of the past managed to develop without the purportedly essential benefit of being explicitly taught how to think. But let us now proceed to consider the contention that thinking skills should constitute a learning objective in themselves and that teachers should be encouraged to teach thinking directly.

According to Fisher, despite the heterogeneity of the thinking skills movement, one objective is common: 'to improve reasoning skills and critical thinking skills by *direct* methods' (Fisher, 1989, p. 39, original italics). Yet it is not clear if it is believed that thinking skills can best be taught, or perhaps can only be taught, by such methods, though good thinkers who have never been through a 'direct' approach obviously falsify the latter suggestion. What is certain, however, is that it is believed that thinking can be taught by methods specifically designed for that purpose and taught independently of any particular content.

By being independent of any specific content, I mean that each thinking skill is thought not to be tied to any particular content, or restricted to any particular subject. It would not, of course, be possible to teach such skills without any content or examples being used at all, but there is no necessity for content from this subject or that; the skills are in a sense free-floating, as indeed they have to be if they are to be subject-independent. Furthermore, some thinking skills programmes use highly abstract material. Cottrell's book, for example, uses only abstract patterns for assessing the 'thinking skills' of comparing and sequencing (2005, pp. 18–19).

The aspect of this so-called direct approach that I highlight here, and develop later, is the devaluing of knowledge. This devaluation can be seen in the following statement, which occurs in a discussion of the need for discrete courses on thinking:

> If the primary aim of education is conceived to be the promotion of children's thinking, then knowledge acquisition has to assume a subsidiary status and thinking must not be taught only as a subcomponent of other activities. (Coles and Robinson, 1989, p. 16)

In fact, it is suggested that when it comes to teaching thinking, subject knowledge gets in the way. McGuinness, for example, says that generic thinking skills 'may get lost in the midst of subject-knowledge-based teaching' (p. 8). Beyer agrees that concentrating on subject knowledge 'so obscures the skills of how to engage in thinking . . . that students simply fail to master these skills' (1985, p. 297). de Bono writes, 'knowledge has its own internal momentum which makes it difficult to pay attention to, or develop, thinking skills' (1978, p. 15). By contrast, a concern for knowledge can, it seems, be energizing and inspiring, and, indeed, the conception of thinking I would advocate is one that is sensitive to and energized by detailed content.

'Detail' may, indeed, serve as a shibboleth in this area; does it evoke Gradgrindian drudgery or a Blakean delight in 'the holiness of the minute particular'? It is my belief that detailed content is not only an essential part of education, but should also be a source of pleasure. For, as Nabokov puts it:

> In art as in science there is no delight without the detail . . .
> All 'general ideas' (so easily acquired, so profitably resold) must necessarily remain but worn out passports allowing their bearers shortcuts from one area of ignorance to another.

In my advocacy of content, I would argue that appropriate, detailed, subject-specific knowledge renders thinking skills redundant. In order to illustrate this redundancy theory, consider the popular general thinking skill of 'comparing' (see, for example, McGuinness Report, p. 5; Baumfield, 2001, p. 9; Cottrell, 2005, pp. 17–18). In order to make a comparison one needs appropriate knowledge of what is to be compared, awareness of the appropriate frame of reference and awareness of the appropriate criteria. For completeness, I would add the need for motivation to carry out the comparison. These three epistemic requirements are likely to be so specific as to have little or no relevance to many other comparisons that one wishes to make. Moreover, given that someone has the motivation, identifies the frame of reference, knows what criteria are relevant and has the appropriate knowledge, what sense could be made of them stating that they cannot make the comparison because they lack the skill? In fact, there is no work for the supposed skill of comparing to do.

I suspect that those who argue for a general skill of 'comparing' are committing the error we noted earlier when considering the naming fallacy. For even if we concede that whenever the concept 'comparing' is properly used, a particular set of conditions will need to be satisfied, it does not follow that there is a corresponding general thinking skill of comparing. Those who say that it does follow are committing themselves to innumerable general thinking skills, such as understanding, believing, knowing, judging, imagining, concluding and theorizing. After all, if the concepts of 'understanding', 'believing', etc. each have a set of conditions for their proper use, then, by parity of reasoning, there must be corresponding general thinking skills. Such a multiplication of entities surely cries out for Occam's razor.

Rather than accept the importance of content, proponents of thinking skills tend to separate content from process and then concentrate on process. They do this because they believe that thinking comprises a number of processes; this is something to which I now turn.

7. Thinking as mental processes

Mental processes are probably illusory; they are certainly elusive. What is true is that belief in them can be educationally harmful.

Most supporters of thinking skills analyse thinking in terms of mental processes. Cottrell, for example, in her popular book on critical thinking, says learning to think critically 'means using mental processes such as attention, categorisation, selection, and judgement' (2005, p. 1). These hypothetical mental events are arrived at by the dubious means of reading backwards from the performance of a task. This approach makes the naming fallacy an ever-present pitfall. For whether we are engaged in chemical analysis or we are analysing a poem, or a chess problem, it may be thought that we are engaged in *one and the same* process. Furthermore, under the influence of the generalizing fallacy, mental processes mistakenly encourage the idea of general transferability. The assumption here is that if a student could be taught to analyse chemical formulae, then she will be able to analyse poems, arguments, etc., etc.

Faith in mental processes also supports the belief (previously encountered in section 2) that thinking can be reduced to a set of pre-specified steps. One of the dangers of this step-by-step approach is that it gets in the way of flashes of insight, leaps, jumps, speculation and the like that are part and parcel of human inquiry. A thinking-skills Newton would have said, 'curse that apple for interrupting my checklist'.

Yet even in very narrow areas of activity (e.g., cooking), such an approach is no guarantee of success. There will always be the need to know what is to count as being relevant (cook until brown – but how brown is brown?) and what it means to get it right (add sugar slowly – but how slowly?). In other words, there must be an understanding of the criteria and standards of a particular activity and these will vary from activity to activity, hence, it is highly unlikely that generic steps or procedures will be appropriate across a range of situations. Of course, it may be possible to find some general prescription that might cover a heterogeneous set of problems, such as 'identify your goal', but when considering a problem with one's marriage, a broken washing machine or an abstruse passage from Hegel, any common set of procedures will surely comprise truistic platitudes of little or no practical worth, as when de Bono recommends 'the operation "Consider All Factors" which we will call CAF' (1978, p. 50). It is not procedures that are important but knowing what is to count as a good reason or a relevant factor within your particular sphere of activity, and this is a matter of having subject-specific knowledge.

Those who believe that thinking can be analysed in terms of mental processes recommend that children become aware of their own mental processes; a recommendation I now consider.

i. Being explicit about mental processes

An essential element in the dominant metacognitive approach to thinking skills is that children should make their thought processes explicit. Throughout the McGuinness Report, and in Government pronouncements too, it is stressed that thinking processes must be made explicit and must be reflected on. Thus, McGuinness says, 'developing thinking requires that children make their own thought processes more explicit thus enabling them to reflect upon their strategies' (p. 5). But what are students supposed to detect and make explicit by means of such introspection? Even a leading cognitive psychologist expresses some doubts: 'if thought is to be defined as information processing that underlies problem-solving, reasoning and decision making, then surprisingly little of this appears to be accessible through introspection' (Evans, 1995, p. 75). There seems no direct introspective access to what McGuinness calls 'higher order thinking' processes (p. 8). In fact, there may be no processes to introspect and make explicit. Despite this, thinking skills programmes insist that it is important for experts, as well as children, to make their thought processes explicit.

ii. Experts' thinking

The McGuinness Report states that, 'powerful learning environments may be powerful precisely because they require the experts to externalise the mental processes they are using' (p. 16). However, research workers in Artificial Intelligence have found (e.g., Chase and Simon, 1973) that thinking expertly within an area may not consist of possessing even subject-specific strategies, but consists in acquiring a vast repertoire of knowledge of typical cases and in being able to recognize a current situation as being similar to those cases. There is certainly much research (see, for example, Hunt, 1989) to support the view that intelligent thinking is not a formal matter but that what is important is possession of detailed subject-specific knowledge. As Dreyfus and Dreyfus put it, 'The expert is simply not following any rules . . . he is recognising thousands of special cases' (1985, p. 108).

Certainly there are no rules or processes for having new ideas. For this, it is necessary to make informed, intelligent guesses. On this basis, what prevents thinking from being a set of skills is that making correct guesses about the unknown cannot be reduced to the operation of known techniques. Imagination is essential here; imagination based on sound knowledge and understanding of the subject, not on general mental processes or metacognitive strategies.

I do, however, have reservations about the formula: novice plus detailed, specific subject knowledge equals expert thinker in that subject. To this simple formula I would add certain virtues, dispositions and circumstances in relation to the particular subject, such as, respect for the subject and its traditions, concern for truth, respect for evidence, patience, determination, insight, imagination, willingness to conjecture, confidence and time, and this list is in no way complete. Still, notwithstanding my reservations about the simple formula, it is questionable whether anyone lacking the elements just listed would acquire the requisite subject knowledge in the first place.

But if the case for specialized knowledge for specialized problems is conceded, what role is left for general thinking skills? It may be argued that general thinking skills are necessary for the development of experts' specialized thinking which then becomes automatic and so does not figure consciously in the expert's thought processes. However, while experts do things like 'defining and clarifying problems' and 'setting priorities' (McGuinness Report, p. 5), there are no corresponding general thinking skills, any more than there are general thinking skills of 'making accurate judgements' or 'deciding what has gone wrong'. There is, then, nothing for experts to employ automatically, and nothing for them to make explicit. Experts saying, 'Now I'm observing, and now I'm hypothesising,' is as useful as, 'Now I'm diagnosing, and now I'm prescribing.'

Even if it were to be conceded that experts did employ thinking skills, and that it was possible to make these explicit, it still would not follow that what is going on in the expert's mind would be helpful to the novice – rather than an irrelevance or even a hindrance – and that such processes are generalizable, rather than idiosyncratic. Suppose an expert did say, 'And now I'm paying attention to the details.' This would be no help to the novice. After all, the novice doesn't know what details are relevant. Finally, those who recommend this approach need to justify the move from *is* to *ought*: from how experts think, to how learners ought to think.

The McGuinness Report's first aim was to get to grips with what is understood by 'thinking skills' (p. 1). Considerable confusion remains however. Is a thinking skill a personal attribute, an act, an outcome of behaviour, a feature of a task, a mental strategy or a mental power? In hope of some clarification, in the following section I examine a number of proposed examples of thinking skills.

8. Examples of general thinking skills

Proposed examples of general thinking skills support the view that there are no such things.

McGuinness tells us that there are 'several general taxonomies' of thinking skills and goes on to say:

> Examples of the different kinds of thinking are: sequencing and ordering information; sorting, classifying, grouping; analysing,

identifying part/whole relationships, comparing and contrasting; making predictions and hypothesising; drawing conclusions, giving reasons for conclusions; distinguishing fact from opinion; determining bias and checking the reliability of evidence; generating new ideas and brainstorming; relating cause and effect, designing a fair test; defining and clarifying problems, thinking up different solutions, setting up goals and sub-goals; testing solutions and evaluating outcomes; planning and monitoring progress towards a goal, revising plans; making decisions, setting priorities, weighing up pros and cons. (p. 5)

This list of thinking skills is based on the one given by Schwartz and Parks (1994), and has been used by a number of other proponents of thinking skills, for example Smith (2002). Smith considers that all thinking skills approaches (e.g., Instrumental Enrichment (Feuerstein), CASE (Adey & Shayer), CORT (de Bono), Philosophy for Children (Lipman), and Accelerated Learning (Smith)) are trying to develop the skills in the above list. But in what sense are these examples of 'different kinds of thinking', and what would be the educational value of identifying opportunities to exercise them across the curriculum? The naming fallacy is at work here. It is true that there are conditions for the correct application of concepts such as comparing (e.g., considering the similarity or dissimilarity of two things), but that does not mean that there is a corresponding unitary thinking skill. In Physical Education we could get the children to watch and compare two forward-rolls; in history we could get the children to read and compare two accounts of the General Strike; in food technology we could get children to taste and compare two soufflés. The children in these three lessons would not, however, be using the same one mental ability and, therefore, there could be no transfer between these different examples of comparing. In other words, it is unlikely that the same transferable skill is being employed when one compares the brain to a computer or one's love to a summer's day. Let us now consider some other proposed examples of general thinking skills.

i. 'Distinguishing fact from opinion'

How do we teach children to distinguish fact from opinion, as McGuinness and others want? Cottrell tells us that an opinion is a belief 'which is not based on proof or substantial evidence' (2005, p. 141). On the other hand, Cottrell says facts can be proved. Rather confusingly, she adds that 'as knowledge of an area increases, facts can later be disproved.' (Ibid.) The main problem here is that the distinction between fact and opinion is (like Cottrell) confused, for while facts are true, some opinions are also true, and while there cannot be an opinion without someone who believes it, many facts are also objects of belief. Perhaps those who try to draw a fact/opinion distinction are seeking to differentiate between facts that are known to be true, that is, facts supported by evidence, and opinions. But, then, many opinions are based on evidence. Maybe the difference lies in the quality of the evidence, which would call for principles of quality assessment. As a way out of these difficulties, McGuinness might recommend getting experts to articulate how they distinguish between known facts and matters of opinion in their areas of expertise. But how would experts make such a distinction? By relying on their subject-specific knowledge? This may seem the obvious answer, and one which wouldn't please the thinking skills lobby, but, in fact, many experts would question the distinction with which they are confronted. Instead of 'known fact', for instance, they may talk of present paradigms, the hypothesis which has best withstood attempts at falsification, the theory that best fits the data, the theory with the greatest explanatory power, the theory that best coheres with previous findings, the theory that exhibits the most elegance and simplicity and so on. Furthermore, Kuhn is probably correct in his claim that there is no algorithm for choosing a theory. Experts, I suspect, are not as McGuinness wants them to be. In short, even if we go along with the distinction drawn, there is no general litmus test for truth and falsity, or for known fact and what is merely believed.

ii. Observation

Observation was claimed to be a general thinking skill as long ago as 1978 (DES, *Primary Education in England*), and is still being advocated (e.g., Higgins and Baumfield, 1998, p. 394 and Cottrell, 2005, p. 4 who claims that critical thinking involves developing the thinking skill of observation). But is observation a general skill? Philosophers and psychologists stress the role of one's interests and/or knowledge in what one observes, while others emphasize the influence of one's values, personality and emotions. All of which, without entailing subjectivism, stresses the individualism and the particularity, not the generality, of observation. Furthermore, as Dearden argues, 'being generally observant seems . . . to be self-contradictory, since to be observant is to be attentive to some specific but easily missed feature in a scene which is always infinite in its variety of descriptions' (1984, pp. 81–82) So, while I do not claim the very idea of general thinking skills is contradictory, maybe some examples can be rejected *a priori*.

iii. 'Checking the Reliability of Evidence'

McGuinness proposes 'checking the reliability of evidence' as a general thinking skill, but the fact that people regularly display astuteness, even brilliance in evaluating evidence in one field, but are abysmal, even non-starters, in others, may tell against claims of generality and transferability here. The point is that evidence is theory-dependent; nothing can be selected or checked as evidence without a prior theory or hypothesis, or at least criteria for what counts as evidence in a particular domain. So, do these evidence-checking 'skills' bring with them the logically prior, bonus general thinking skill of being able to hypothesize across domains? How desirable; how improbable. Improbable or not, McGuinness includes 'making predictions and hypothesising' in her 'general taxonomy of thinking' (p. 5).

Maybe the Generalizing Fallacy is again at work, prompting the conclusion that if someone can check evidence in one murder case, then she has the wider skill of checking evidence in any criminal investigation or, wider still and wider, the skill of checking evidence anywhere and everywhere.

iv. 'Being systematic'

Another general thinking skill mentioned by McGuinness, and included in other lists of such skills (e.g., Higgins and Baumfield, 1998, p. 394), is that of 'being systematic'. This illustrates another error common in this area and one I considered earlier: confusing a disposition, virtue or personality trait with a skill. Central to being systematic is being disposed to act in certain ways, but one may have a skill without being inclined to exercise it. Others who are guilty of this confusion include Pratzner, who has listed as 'transferable skills', 'kindness', 'honesty' and 'loyalty' (1978, p. 7), and Wallis, who lists 'self-confidence' and 'coping with uncertainty' (1996, p. 3).

I believe the objections to general thinking skills are sufficiently powerful to cast serious doubt on their educational value and even on their existence. I now consider more particularly the educational dangers of characterizing thinking in terms of such skills.

9. The dangers

The present preoccupation with thinking skills is educationally dangerous.

The thinking skills movement rightly takes the opportunity to castigate the teaching of inert facts (the 'Trivial Pursuits' view of knowledge) and procedures divorced from their rationale or application (e.g., that $a^2 - b^2 = (a + b)(a - b)$ can be applied to a problem such as $17^2 - 13^2$). The problem is that this disparagement is extended to all subject knowledge.

i. Disparagement of subject knowledge

There is a real danger that subject knowledge will be seen as nothing more than material on which to practise skills, or even as something that gets in the way of the real business of education: thinking skills.

Subject knowledge, however, is far more important than those who espouse thinking skills can allow. The truth is that errors committed in making judgements come in many forms. Some, probably most, are factual and need to be rectified by supplying learners with, or enabling them to acquire, the correct information. Some errors are the result of failure to appreciate the force of appropriate credentials for a belief. Other errors may occur because of an inability to follow specific procedures, such as a historian incorrectly implementing radiocarbon dating methods. But of course all of these are closely associated with subjects and, therefore, will be subject-specific. One cannot divorce thinking from the content of what is being thought about. Subject matter will largely determine what is to count as good thinking in any particular area. Furthermore, subject-specific content will develop mental abilities that are peculiar to that subject.

One common misconception in this area involves confusing knowledge with isolated bits of information. Professor Sir Graham Hills tells us 'heads crammed with knowledge are no longer as desirable as they once were. Such is the power of databases and information networks that knowledge is instantly accessible at the press of a button' (*The Guardian* 18 September 1990). A more recent example is provided by Mike Cresswell, head of Britain's largest examination board. He said that exams were increasingly designed to test thinking skills and to reduce the amount of knowledge students need. The reason he gave for this was that 'there is so much information that is rapidly accessible.' Mr Cresswell added that 'the more important skills' concern 'what you do with the information, how you process it' (*Daily Telegraph*, 16 August 2008). This is the computer programmer's view of knowledge as inert data that have to be manipulated and worked on. This misconception allows skills, conceived of as being active, practical and useful, to be favourably contrasted with knowledge, which is represented as being passive, theoretical and inert. But knowledge is not inert; it is actively involved in the way a person sees and interacts with the world. There is another sense in which such knowledge must not be 'inert', in that it should involve commitment and caring; it is a matter of being on the inside of and appreciating a form of thought, as opposed to viewing it externally and with detachment. The issue of detachment raises another threat posed by thinking skills: the depersonalizing and neutralizing of thought, to which I now turn.

ii. Thinking as impersonal and value-neutral

de Bono, writing of his teaching thinking course, says, 'The aim is to produce a "detached" thinking skill so that the thinker can use his skill in the most effective way. A thinker ought to be able to say, "My thinking on this is not very good," or "My thinking performance is poor in this area," without feeling that his ego is threatened' (de Bono, 1978, p. 52). But thinking is not an incidental skill like being able to swim. Thinking is constitutive of our humanity and of who we are, and is related to a commitment to truth. At stake here are the complex connections between knowledge, virtue and education. Thinking skills are often presented as tools, thus emphasizing their separation from our dispositions, our values and our personality; tools reveal little about the nature of those who use them. However, thought, knowledge and one's orientation towards the world are connected. The self needs an integrated perspective in which there is a harmony of thought and action in the light of morality. This is threatened if thinking is reduced to a set of impersonal techniques.

Most thinking skills programmes are reductive and instrumental. They concentrate in the main on the logical assessment of arguments and means-ends reasoning in which the goals are given. In fact, ends and values present difficulties for thinking skills courses. In his highly influential paper on critical thinking skills, Robert Ennis writes: 'the judging of value statements is deliberately excluded' (1962, p. 84). Despite appreciating the importance of values, Ennis found it impossible to incorporate them into his 'pure skills' conception of critical thinking. The exclusion of values obviously weakens the concept; the ability to think critically about ends and values in particular subject areas is a most desirable and important educational objective and an indispensable attribute for any critical thinker.

Most proponents of thinking skills exhibit the same sort of ethical detachment. de Bono, for example, writes, 'in teaching thinking skills one is not trying to teach morals' (de Bono, 1978, p. 69). de Bono then declares that right thinking is quite separate from right living. However, as Socrates stressed, teachers should not be indifferent to the uses others may put what they have been taught. Indeed, for Socrates, to educate was to be committed to the moral improvement of one's students, to bring them into the light of the knowledge of what is right and good. Without a concern for values, thinking skills may merely enable students to produce sophistical rationalizations in support of their prejudices.

This concern for values should embrace the intellectual virtues. The present enthusiasm for teaching thinking could provide a welcome opportunity to focus upon these. McGuinness gestures in this direction when she says, 'Developing higher order thinking may have as much to do with creating a disposition to be a good thinker as it has to do with acquiring specific skills' (p. 6). Unfortunately this point is not developed; unfortunate, but foreseeable given McGuinness's strong support for a skills approach. An impediment to such an approach embracing the intellectual virtues is its apparent lack of enthusiasm for truth.

iii. A lack of enthusiasm for truth

As far as I can see the McGuinness Report does not contain the word 'truth'. This may be the result of the report's commitment to constructivism: the view that 'knowledge is actively created and constructed by learners' (p. 5). If, however, knowledge is *true* belief for which we have appropriate credentials, then we cannot simply construct knowledge as we wish. It is, however, a common feature of courses in thinking skills that they eschew any commitment to truth. It is claimed, for example, that the use of thinking skills does 'not require the determination of the truth of a complex informational issue' (Quinn, 1994, p. 108), and that the outcome of thinking skills will not involve 'determining the truth of issues' (Ibid.). Yet, this lack of enthusiasm for truth is, I suspect, more pragmatic than metaphysical. For whereas it may seem plausible to argue for the thinking skill of spotting logical fallacies, the notion of there being a general transferable skill of truth-spotting or truth-discovering is much less credible.

There is also a lack of engagement with truth in the currently popular Advanced Level subject, Critical Thinking Skills. Practitioners to whom I have spoken consider the course to be little more than English comprehension exercises. They also complain that students are discouraged from speculating or going beyond the given information (see OCR Examiners' Report, June 2006, for example question 22). The type of thinking encouraged by Critical Thinking Skills seems to be destructive rather than constructive and critical of arguments rather than of premises or conclusions. It encourages the view that intelligent thinking is synonymous with logical thinking. For as one textbook puts it, 'to think critically means that we are able to think in a logical fashion – in straight lines, as it were' (Jones, 1997, p. 2). Argument is considered to be the essence of thinking, and yet our thinking is often not argumentative or rule-bound. In fact, much of our intelligent thinking is intuitive, creative and speculative. As regards truth, Miller is surely right in his assertion that 'only those who are impressed by style rather that substance could be convinced by an argument, rather than by what it is the premises assert' (2005, p. 66). What should persuade us of the truth of the conclusion is the truth of the premises.

Computers, of course, are not concerned with the truth of the data they manipulate, and the computerization of thought is the final danger I highlight.

iv. The computerization of thought

Many of my misgivings about thinking skills may be summarized as worries about the computerization of thought. Cognitive psychologists like McGuinness tend to view the brain as a computer. Computers manipulate data according to rules; problems must be explicitly defined and broken down, and then procedures applied. This model of thought can lead to the illusion that all intelligent thinking is logical and rule-governed.

Human thought and behaviour doesn't fit this model. Much of our thinking is intuitive and speculative. And even if some behaviour can be described *as if* it is rule-following, the proposed underlying rules play no part in the behaviour. In order to catch a ball that is bounced off a wall, I don't need to know the rule: go to the point where the angle of incidence is equal to the angle of reflection in a plane where the flatness of the trajectory is a function of the impact velocity divided by the coefficient of friction. Nor is such a calculation going on as an implicit mental process. Psychoanalysis, so far as I know, cannot get ball-catchers to relate this rule under hypnosis.

Another difficulty with this model is the notion of explicitly defining a problem. A definition will use language (with its inevitable ambiguities) which will pick out some salient aspects but leave others implicit. Furthermore, a computer would need to consider all possible implications of an act, both intended and unintended, and then differentiate between relevant and irrelevant implications. Fortunately, we do not think mechanistically but intuitively. Logic is of no use here; it is by understanding content and context that we have insights concerning what is reasonable or likely. There is a parallel with understanding a foreign language where 'the great thing is to learn to cut out the alternative meanings which are logically possible; you are always liable to bring them up till you have "grasped the spirit" of the language, and then you know they aren't meant' (Empson, 1977, p. 13). Unfortunately, there is no general thinking skill of grasping the spirit of things.

The computer model of thought increases the danger that content will be misrepresented as data to be atomized into components and manipulated into whatever construction the thinker wishes. Hence, thinking skills, and those who possess them, are seen to be external to the content upon which thinking skills are deployed. This separates not only process from content, but also thinker from context and so from the world. I argue for a very different orientation: that form and order are not imposed upon, but emerge from content and context. We should strive for a sensitive and receptive engagement with content.

Finally, as an example of how this model of thought is antithetical to educationally important activities, we may consider conversation. Conversation is particularly apt as it is also a fruitful metaphor for education itself. Oakeshott refers to conversation as 'an unrehearsed intellectual adventure' (1962, p. 198). It is not merely about sending and receiving information. Conversation doesn't shuffle and manipulate information; it enables something new to be created. In this way conversation can change the way that participants see the world and how they see and feel about themselves and each other.

10. Conclusion

Some of the most important elements of our thought and nature are dismissed.

The Government's inclusion of thinking skills in the National Curriculum is surely ill-thought out and hasty. As the McGuinness Report itself cautions, 'considerable evaluation work remains to be done' (p. 1). Even supporters and exponents of thinking skills disagree about what these entities are and how they can be taught. As an example, consider Alister Smith who is, according to the *Times Educational Supplement*, 'the guru of Accelerated Learning', and has three of his books on the Government's list of recommended resources for teaching thinking. But, despite being a leading player in the thinking skills game, Smith responds to his own question: 'can thinking skills be taught – is it worth the effort?' by saying, 'the current research evidence as to how and when and for what duration is confused and, I would argue, contaminated by poor controls' (2002, p. 2). This present account, in keeping with other writings and research findings, raises doubts about the educational value of thinking skills and their very existence. For instance, the *Teaching Thinking Skills Report* to the Scottish Executive, after noting that 'evaluation studies are inconclusive' (Wilson, 2000, p. 39), concluded that 'Given the paucity of evidence, it would, perhaps, be fairer to conclude that "the jury is still out on this particular issue"' (Ibid.). Also consider Roy van den Brink-Budgen, a former Chief Examiner in Critical Thinking, who has developed assessment materials for critical thinking skills for over 20 years and is the author of very popular books on the subject. He too has expressed doubts about whether thinking skills are generalizable. In November 2006 he said, regarding general thinking skills, 'we should retain some scepticism until the evidence is more than anecdotal' (2006, p. 4).

As well as being over-hasty, there is also an inconsistency in the National Curriculum embracing thinking skills. The National Curriculum is founded upon subjects viewed as self-contained units, whereas the thinking skills movement is dismissive of such subject autonomy. In fact, there is often hostility towards subject areas or domains. The movement encourages the view that we need to learn to think *in general*, that such thinking can be taught without content specificity and, indeed, that school subjects, with their accumulated knowledge and practices, run counter to such teaching. In the end this could lead to a forced marriage that can't last: the promotion of thinking for oneself joined with the promulgation of ignorance. You may have met the progeny of such a coupling. Enough said.

Regrettably, it is not just the importance of school subjects that is dismissed by supporters of thinking skills, but also some of the most important elements of our thought and nature. These include truth, knowledge, understanding and values. By reducing thinking to a checklist of skills, a vital fact is ignored: that education should engage with the personality of both teacher and taught, and that teaching is not a technology but a moral activity involving complex relationships which are in principle irreducible and unpredictable.

What, then, are the implications of this inquiry for curriculum planning? McGuinness believes that 'higher order thinking' will not be developed by 'subject knowledge-based teaching' (1990, p. 301). If true, McGuinness's belief would make earlier generations of competent thinkers, let alone great thinkers of the past, educational miracles – millions of intellectual Lazaruses. But there is no need to jettison curricula that emphasize subject knowledge for the sake of producing good thinkers. On the contrary, such curricula are the only ones that will produce good thinkers, because thinking is always thinking about something in particular and within a particular context. The National Curriculum is correct, therefore, to emphasize the importance of content, context and subject-based abilities, that is, to stress subject knowledge, both propositional and procedural.

Curriculum subjects embody traditions of inquiry (Oakeshott's 'conversations of mankind') and important concepts, ideas and procedures for exploring and understanding experience. The National Curriculum provides the opportunity for the sort of thinking and understanding I advocate. In the teaching of mathematics, for instance, there is an emphasis on grasping the 'language' of mathematics: understanding mathematical ideas and concepts.

As another example let us consider science. The National Curriculum recognizes that in order to develop thinking in science it is necessary to be initiated into a particular style of thinking. This requires knowledge of scientific facts, theories and techniques. There is also the need to know classificatory rules and standards of evaluation, and to appreciate the quality and purpose of scientific explanations.

The National Curriculum for science (Qualifications and Curriculum Authority, 2008b) begins by talking about science exciting 'pupils' curiosity about phenomena and events in the world around them', and goes on to say that science 'satisfies this curiosity with knowledge'. Some of this knowledge will be propositional as in Key Stage 1, Sc1: Light and sound – 'Pupils should be taught that sounds travel away from sources, getting fainter as they do so'; or in Key Stage 2, Sc2: Life processes and living things – 'Pupils should be taught that the heart acts as a pump to circulate the blood through vessels around the body.' Other knowledge will be more procedural, as in Key Stage 1, Sc1: Scientific enquiry, where 'pupils are taught to ask questions [for example, 'How?' 'Why?' 'What will happen if . . .?'] and decide how they might find answers to them'; and in Key stage 2, Sc1: Scientific enquiry, which states that pupils should be taught to consider evidence, evaluate, observe and hypothesize. But these are not presented as general skills; they are scientific abilities taught within specific scientific contexts and employing 'scientific knowledge and understanding'.

Are there any aspects of the general thinking skills approach that could be compatible with a curriculum based on subject knowledge? One possibility might be if metacognition, instead of concentrating on mental strategies employed to manipulate content, could focus on self-monitoring directed towards developing certain habits of mind; concerning a general spirit of thinking, rather than general thinking skills. Some of the intellectual virtues I have in mind are: respect for truth; concern for accuracy; openness and charity towards different ideas, while maintaining a critical spirit; determination; willingness to conjecture; patience with the frustrations and *longueur* of learning and confidence to question authorities and tackle difficult questions. Dearden

(1984, p. 106) gives other examples, including: 'humility to recognise a need to learn, restraining one's natural passion for certainty, and controlling one's natural impulsiveness to believe what is immediately congenial to believe'.

What then of Philosophy? Well, this critique is philosophical and Philosophy is thought by some to provide general thinking skills (see, for example, Fisher, ch. 6, 1990). Can I reconcile my belief in the benefits of Philosophy with my criticism of general thinking skills? Or am I rather like an atheist who believes in miracles?

The answer is that the benefits of Philosophy can be supported without recourse to the problematic notion of general thinking skills, by stressing Philosophy's breadth. Philosophy courses should involve coming to appreciate the different kinds of reasonings, assumptions and problems that operate in different areas. Some problems, for instance, overlap a number of areas. Take the distinction between facts and values; students who have studied this problem may be justified in feeling that they can say something about a problem in ethics, aesthetics or politics.

If Philosophy is to help in this way it needs to be broad and it needs to look at problems that occur in different fields. The high degree of abstraction required here probably makes this type of Philosophy unsuitable for schoolchildren, though perhaps it could be tackled in the sixth form. Younger children should concentrate on gaining a thorough grounding in the main curriculum areas. This is necessary because the context-dependency of problems means that without detailed subject-specific knowledge even the most rounded of philosophers will not be able to tackle them.

Philosophy, then, is not a general admission ticket to any area of knowledge; an understanding of the area under consideration is essential. There again, a subject must have philosophical aspects in order for any philosophical critique to gain purchase. In short, Philosophy does not provide the equivalent of intellectual bus passes to all areas. It doesn't even provide passes to all its own parts – a philosopher of science may have little or nothing to contribute to a discussion on aesthetics. Still, as Philosophy operates at a high level of generality, it is likely that most areas will have elements that come within the purview of Philosophy, but some will have more than others. Hence, Philosophy will have more to say about thinking than plumbing. So don't phone a philosopher if your water pipes burst.

Yet this apparent lack of immediate practicality should not be seen as a weakness or as a reason for dismissing philosophical criticism. Sound curricular proposals should be able to withstand philosophic scrutiny. It is my conclusion that recent curricular recommendations concerning general thinking skills cannot withstand such scrutiny. The least that learners deserve is that they are not forced to pursue courses that assume entities which have not been adequately accounted for or whose existence has not been adequately established.

Of course we want students to think imaginatively, creatively and to solve problems. But, as Whitehead observed, 'education is a patient process of the mastery of details, minute by minute, hour by hour, day by day. There is no royal road to learning through an airy path of brilliant generalisations' (1959, p. 10) or, we could add, by supposed general thinking skills, even with government endorsement.

References

Anderson, J. R. (1993), *Rules of the Mind*, Hillsdale, NY:Lawrence Erlbaum Associates.

Bailin, S. and Siegel, H. (2003), 'Critical thinking', in N. Blake, P. Smeyers, R. Smith and P. Standish (eds), *The Blackwell Guide to Philosophy of Education*, Blackwell: Oxford, pp. 181–193.

Barrow, R. (1987), 'Skill talk', *Journal of Philosophy of Education*, 21.2, 187–199.

Baumfield, V. (2001), 'Ill Thought Out Thinking Skills'. *Teaching Thinking*, Winter 2001, issue 6.

Beyer, B. (1985), 'Teaching critical thinking: A Direct Approach', *Social Education*, 49.4, 297–303.

Blagg, N., Ballinger, M. and Gardner, R. (1988), *Somerset Thinking Skills Course*, Oxford: Basil Blackwell.

Bobbitt, F. (1926), *How to Make a Curriculum*, Boston: Hougton Mifflin.

Brink-Budgen, Roy van den (2006), *The Skeptic Express*, Nov. 06, 1–10.

Chase, W. G. and Simon, H. A. (1973), 'Perception in chess', *Cognitive Psychology*, 4, 55–81.

City and Guilds, (1991), *Diploma of Vocational Education Handbook*, London: City & Guilds.

Coles, A. and Robinson, W. D. (eds) (1989), *Teaching Thinking*, Bristol: Bristol Classical Press.

Cottrell, S. (2005), *Critical Thinking Skills*, Basingstoke: Macmillan.

Davis, A. (1996), *Assessment, Accountability and Transfer*, unpublished paper given at Cambridge Philosophy of Education Society.

Dearden, R. F. (1984), *Theory and Practice in Education*, London: Routledge & Kegan Paul.

de Bono, E. (1978), *Teaching Thinking*, Harmondsworth: Penguin.

de Bono, E. (1996), *Teach Yourself to Think*, Harmondsworth: Penguin.

DES, (1978), *Primary Education in England*, London: HMSO.

DfEE, (1999), *From Thinking Skills to Thinking Classrooms: A review and evaluation of approaches for developing pupils' thinking*, Research Report RR115, London: HMSO.

DfES, (2004a), *Primary National Strategy*, www.standards.dfes.gov.uk/primary/

—(2004b), *Teaching and Learning in the Foundation Subjects* www.standards.dfes.gov.uk/keystage3/casestudies/cs_fs_teach_learn

—(2005), *Leading in Learning: Developing Thinking*, www.standards.dfes.gov.uk/secondary/keystage3/all/respub/ws_lil_ts

—(2008), *Standards Site*, www.standards.dfes.gov.uk/thinkingskills

Dreyfus, H. L. and Dreyfus, S. (1985), *Mind over Machine*, New York: Macmillan.

Empson, W. (1977), *Seven Types of Ambiguity*, Harmondsworth: Penguin.

Ennis, R. H. (1962), 'A concept of critical thinking', *Harvard Education Review*, 32.1: 81–111.

Evans, J. St. B. T. (1995), 'Thinking and reasoning', in C. C. French, and A. M. Colman (eds), *Cognitive Psychology*, London: Longman, pp. 58–77.

FEU, (1982), *Basic Skills*, London: DES/FEU.

Feuerstein, R., Rand, Y., Hoffman, M. D. and Miller, R. (1980), *Instrumental Enrichment: An Intervention for Cognitive Modifiability*, Baltimore: University Park Press.

Fisher, A. (ed.) (1988), *Critical Thinking*, Norwich: UEA.

Fisher, A. (1989), 'Critical thinking', in A. Coles and W. D. Robinson, (eds), *Teaching Thinking*, Bristol: Bristol Classical Press, pp. 37–45.

Fisher, R. (1990), *Teaching Children to Think*, Oxford: Blackwell.

—(2002), *Thinking through History*, Cambridge: Chris Kington Publishing.

Goodman, N. (1970), 'Seven strictures on similarity', in L. Foster and J. Swanson (eds), *Experience and Theory*, London, Duckworth, pp. 19–29.

Hardy, T. (1931), *The Dynasts*, London, Macmillan.

Henry, D. P. (1984), *That Most Subtle Question*, Manchester: Manchester University Press.

Higgins, S. and Baumfield, V. (1998), 'A defence of teaching general thinking skills', *Journal of Philosophy of Education*, 32.3, 391–398.

Hunt, G. M. K. (1989), 'Skills, facts and artificial intelligence', in A. Coles and W. D. Robinson (eds), *Teaching Thinking*, Bristol: Bristol Classical Press, pp. 23–29.

James, W. (1890), *Principles of Psychology*, New York: Henry Holt.

Jones, H. M. (1997), *An Introduction to Critical Thinking*, London: Social Science Press.

Kripke, S. A. (1993), *Wittgenstein on Rules and Private Language*, Oxford: Blackwell.

Lave, J. and Wenger, E. (1991), *Situated Learning: Legitimate Peripheral Participation*, New York: Cambridge University Press.

McGuinness, C. (1990), 'Talking about thinking: The role of metacognition in teaching thinking', in K. J.Gilhooly, M. T. G. Keane, R. H. Logie, and G. Erdos (eds), *Lines of Thinking, Vol. 2*, Chichester: Wiley, pp. 301–312.

Mentis, M. & Dunn-Bernstein, M. (2008), *Mediated Learning* (2nd Ed.) Thousand Oaks, CA: Corwin Press.

Miller, D. W. (2005), 'Do we reason when we think we reason, or do we think?', *Learning for Democracy*, 1.3: 57–71.

MSC, (1984), *Core Skills in YTS*, Sheffield: MSC.

Norris, S.P. (1990), 'Thinking about critical thinking', in J. E. McPeck, *Teaching Critical Thinking*, New York: Routledge, pp. 67–74.

Oakeshott, M. (1962), *Rationalism in Politics*, London: Methuen.

Onetcenter, (2008) *online.onetcenter.org/skills*. (Accessed 16 June 2009).

Perkins, D. N. (1985), 'General cognitive skills: why not?', in J. W. Segal, S. F. Chipman and R. Glaser (eds), *Thinking and Learning Skills, vol.1, Relating Instruction to Research*, Hillsdale, NY: Lawrence Erlbaum Associates, pp. 339–363.

Pratzner, F. C. (1978), *Occupational Adaptability and Transferable Skills*, Columbus: Ohio State University Press.

Qualifications and Curriculum Authority (2008a), *Key Skills*. http://www.qca.org.uk/qca_6444.aspx (Accessed 16 June 2009)

Qualifications and Curriculum Authority, (2008b), *National Curriculum*, http://curriculum.qca.org.uk (Accessed 16 June 2009)

Quinn, V. (1994), 'In defence of critical thinking as a subject', *Journal of Philosophy of Education*, 28.1: 101–111.

Ruthven, K. (1988) 'Ability stereotyping in mathematics', *Educational Studies in Mathematics*, 18: 243–253.

Ryle, G. (1949), *The Concept of Mind*, London: Hutchinson.

—(1979), *On Thinking*, Oxford: Basil Blackwell.

Scheffler, I. (1965), *Conditions of Knowledge*, Chicago: Scott, Foresman & Co.

Schwartz, R. and Parks, D. (1994), *Infusing the Teaching of Critical and Creative Thinking in Elementary Instruction*, Pacific Grove, CA: Critical Thinking Press.

Scriven, M. (1990), 'Foreword', in McPeck, J. E., *Teaching Critical Thinking*, New York, Routledge.

Shayer, M. and Adey, P. (2002), *Learning Intelligence*, Buckingham: Open University Press.

Siegel, H. (1990), 'McPeck, informal logic, and the nature of critical thinking', in J. E. McPeck (ed.), *Teaching Critical Thinking*, New York: Routledge, pp. 75–85.

Singley, M. K. (1995), 'Promoting transfer through model tracing', in A. Keough, J. L. Lupart, and A. Marini (eds), *Teaching for Transfer*, Hillsdale, NY:Lawrence Erlbaum Associates, pp. 69–93

Singley, M. K. and Anderson, J. R. (1989), *The Transfer of Cognitive Skill*, Cambridge, MA: Harvard University Press.

Smith, A. (2002), Foreword in M. Rockett and S. Percival, *Thinking for Learning*, Stafford: Network Educational Press.

Sternberg, R. J. (Ed), (1982), *Handbook of Human Intelligence*, Cambridge, Cambridge University Press.

Urmson, J. O. (1970), 'Polymorphous concepts', in O. P. Wood and G. Pitcher (eds), *Ryle*, Basingstoke: Macmillan, pp. 249–266.

Wallis, M. (1996), 'Personal transferable skills', *Forum*, University of Warwick, 3, 3.

Whitehead, A. N. (1959), *The Aims of Education and Other Essays*, London: Ernest Benn.

Wilson, V. (2000), *Can Thinking Skills Be Taught?* Edinburgh: Scottish Council for Research in Education.

Wittgenstein, L. (1958), *Philosophical Investigations*, Oxford: Basil Blackwell.

On Thinking Skills

Harvey Siegel

Chapter Outline

1. Introduction — 51
2. Problems with thinking of thinking as a skill — 54
3. 'The myth of general transferability' — 61
4. The 'direct' teaching of thinking and content/subject matter knowledge — 75
5. Mental processes and general thinking skills — 78
6. The educational dangers of thinking of thinking in terms of skills — 80
7. Conclusion — 82
   References — 83
   Further reading — 84

1. Introduction

The topic of 'thinking skills' is complex, with several interwoven layers. Are there any such things as thinking skills? If so, are they rightly thought of as *skills*, or rather as abilities, dispositions, habits of mind or something else? Are they the sort of thing that can be taught? Are they subject-specific, or more general? Are they more or less important educationally than subject-matter knowledge? Stephen Johnson's chapter treats all these questions and more. While I have considerable sympathy with much of Johnson's discussion, I worry that it is based far too heavily on the British government's understanding of thinking skills as manifested in the British National Curriculum and its supporting documents. I agree with much of Johnson's critique of that understanding, including his trenchant criticisms of both the language used in its articulation and the policies flowing from it. But one must distinguish philosophical questions about the existence and character of thinking skills from the particular understanding of thinking skills manifested in the policies and implementation of the British National Curriculum. In what follows I try to draw the relevant distinctions and articulate and assess the relevant claims, theses and policy recommendations. On many of them I agree with Johnson's assessments, though not always for the same reasons.

I should note that I am not British, and have at best only a passing acquaintance with the British educational establishment. So much of what I say may be seen by some readers as the reactions of an uninformed outsider. There is considerable truth in this charge. Still, as the questions raised go beyond Britain's borders, perhaps an outsider's perspective is not wholly out of place.

I note in passing that some philosophers might think it rather easy, philosophically uninteresting, and so not worthwhile to criticize the 'theoretical underpinning' (Johnson 2010, p. 5 – all untethered page references below are to this work) of government reports written by non-philosophers. I mention this objection just in order to dismiss it: if indeed an influential policy document rests on untenable philosophical assumptions, presuppositions or substantive theses, it is surely important to point this out, and it equally surely falls within the purview of philosophers of education to demonstrate that untenability and to expose and critique the problematic policies that flow from it.

Johnson's critique is multifaceted, and it will be worthwhile to lay it out briefly and in broad strokes first before discussing particular criticisms and issues in more detail. His main announced target is thinking skills, but there are many ancillary others: transferability, generalizability, mental processes, an unwise lack of attention to knowledge in curricula that emphasize skills, and of course thinking itself and various approaches to teaching (for) it. Johnson sensibly focuses to a large extent on the influential McGuinness Report (DFEE 1999) – '[r]arely, if ever, has so concise a report had so considerable an influence on educational policy' (p. 4) – and some of its 'key conclusions: that thinking is best conceived of as a skill; that thinking skills should be made explicit; that students must be explicitly and directly taught thinking skills; that transfer is crucially important; [and] that students should make explicit, and reflect upon, their own thought processes and cognitive strategies (a metacognitive approach)' (p. 5). He sets out to challenge particular 'theoretical underpinnings' of the report, calling into question the report's 'construing thinking as a skill, the conviction that thinking is a matter of processing information, and belief in general thinking skills, such as analysing and hypothesizing' (p. 5). According to Johnson's analysis of the conception of thinking 'enshrined in the National Curriculum' (p. 9), thinking is conceived by the contemporary official British educational establishment as a skill and/or a mental process that is, at least to a significant extent, general and transferable. So conceived, educational efforts aimed at enhancing student thinking should focus on teaching students thinking skills explicitly and directly, and encouraging students to reflect, meta-cognitively, upon their own thinking. On this picture, skills are active, while knowledge is passive and inert; skills are analysable into sub-components; and explicit educational attention to these skills and sub-skills can enhance student thinking. Johnson challenges this entire conception, and I take up the several features just listed in what follows. A considerable portion of his critique concerns the pedagogical recommendations of the McGuinness report. In particular, Johnson challenges the claims that in teaching students how to think well, thinking skills should be made explicit; that students should be taught thinking skills explicitly and directly; and that students should make explicit, and reflect upon, their own thought processes and cognitive strategies. All these matters, both metaphysical and pedagogical, are taken up below.

In the course of examining Johnson's critique, I briefly defend my own positive view – which I think falls between the enthusiastic embrace of general thinking skills in the National Curriculum that Johnson effectively criticizes, and Johnson's strong rejection of such skills – according to which there are indeed some educationally important thinking/reasoning skills or abilities, that are general in the sense that they can be applied to many diverse situations and subject matters.

2. Problems with thinking of thinking as a skill

One thing to note at the outset: if thinking is a skill, it's not a single skill, as Johnson's examples of the candidate skills of analysing and hypothesizing, cited above, make clear. While Johnson sometimes writes as though his target is the single skill, thinking, it is clear both that that target admits of a plural rendering and that Johnson frequently has the plural rendering in his sights, and I henceforth proceed on the assumption that it is the idea of thinking as a set of distinct skills that Johnson sets out to challenge. When, following Johnson, I use or mention 'thinking skill' in the singular, I hope the reader will take it as convenient shorthand for the plural 'thinking skills'.

Johnson's objections to thinking of thinking as a skill are both metaphysical (there aren't any; whatever thinking is, it's not a skill) and pedagogical. They include the following:

(i) Unlike virtues and character traits, failure to exhibit a skill does not indicate a lack of that skill. (One may have the skills of swimming, bicycle riding and potato peeling, but for any number of reasons fail to exercise them, either on a given occasion or systemically over time.) Virtues, character traits and dispositions are different: failure to exhibit them in appropriate circumstances counts against one's having them. If one fails to manifest kindness or generosity, or fails to seek evidence against one's cherished beliefs, either in given instances or systematically, one's claim to have them – to be kind, generous, or disposed to seek contrary evidence – may be legitimately called into question. (p. 8)

Niceties aside, I agree with Johnson here. But what has this got to do with thinking skills? The worry is ultimately pedagogical: that if we think of thinking as a skill, 'we may lose sight of the dispositional side of thinking, overlooking that thinking is continuous with our humanity and constitutive of it' (p. 8). I agree that this would be a bad thing. But of course to say that we *may* lose sight of this is not to say that we *will* or *must* lose sight of it. As Johnson puts it, this is an 'educational danger' (p. 7), and it is open to the advocate of thinking skills to take the worry on board without giving up the idea that thinking is a skill. She can simply say 'thinking is a skill, but let's not forget that it also has a dispositional side.' It must be admitted that if the 'dispositional side of thinking' is acknowledged by that advocate, and if skills and dispositions are thought to be fundamentally distinct and non-overlapping, then she cannot hold that thinking is *only* or *wholly* a matter of skill. But this still leaves the advocate with plenty of options: she can deny that thinking of thinking as a skill precludes acknowledgement of its dispositional side; she can acknowledge the danger Johnson mentions and make room for avoiding it in her account and/or in her pedagogical and policy recommendations; and so on. So Johnson's point, while I think correct, is by itself not yet determinative. Perhaps more seriously, we should ask why virtues have entered the discussion at all. Is Johnson suggesting that instead of thinking of thinking as a skill, we should think of it as a virtue? This would of course be a very large (and on the face of it implausible) claim, in need of much development, clarification and defence.

(ii) Johnson considers imperative and interrogative 'linguistic tests' for distinguishing between skills, virtues and knowledge. Taking up the imperative test first, he writes: 'I would propose that a necessary, though not a sufficient, condition of something being a skill is that it must make good linguistic sense to tell someone to do it' (p. 9). Johnson suggests that since it does not make good linguistic sense to tell someone to know, believe, understand or appreciate something, these cannot (according to this test) be rightly regarded as skills. Whether or not this test is a good one, though, 'thinking' is not on Johnson's list, and whether or not it might be rightly put on the list is open to debate, since it does seem to make good linguistic sense when a parent tells a child to 'think about what you've done,' 'think about how doing that will make Johnny feel,' 'think how happy you'll be if you put in the effort and make the team (or honour role),' 'don't be discouraged, think positively,' etc. There are subtleties lurking here, not least because relevant distinctions can be drawn between 'thinking about' and 'thinking that'. Nevertheless, Johnson's imperative test is inconclusive until we can see our way clear to adding 'thinking' to his list of non-actions/non-skills.

He next considers Scheffler's interrogative test: 'in answers to the question "What are you doing?" it makes good [linguistic] sense to reply, "I am swimming", or "I am typing", but not "I am knowing", or "I am believing"' (p. 9). Notice again that 'thinking' is not on the list of activities ruled out from being skills by Scheffler's test. Moreover, it seems perfectly fine, linguistically, to answer the question with 'I am thinking (e.g., about how best to respond to Johnson's point about Scheffler's test).' So again, these linguistic tests seem inconclusive: they seem to permit thinking of thinking as a skill.

(iii) The McGuinness Report's conception of thinking as a skill 'places thinking firmly on the side of "knowing-how" rather than "knowing that"' (p. 10), which distinction, Johnson argues, 'can be educationally unhelpful', in that it 'may . . . divorce beliefs from actions, and drive a wedge between mental processes, which are taken to be active, and knowledge, which is taken to be inert' (p. 10). Johnson points out that 'this passivity-grounded and reductive view of propositional knowledge' is 'consistent with the information-processing model of the brain, which is such a dominant paradigm in many thinking skills programmes' (p. 10). We shall return to Johnson's objections to viewing thinking in terms of mental processes and information processing below.

In addition to separating belief from action and mental processes from knowledge, Johnson also objects to thinking of thinking as a skill on the grounds that the exercise of skills typically requires neither thinking nor understanding, and indeed, that 'to have mastered a skill usually means to be able to exercise it without thinking' (p. 10). One can and typically does ride a bicycle skilfully without thinking about exercising the skill, and one can and typically does ride skilfully without understanding the relevant physics.

These objections – that an active thinking vs. passive knowledge distinction may be educationally unhelpful; and that the exercise of a skill typically does not involve thinking, and so it seems inappropriate to think of thinking itself as such a skill ('she exercised her thinking skills without thinking,' or, more dramatically, 'she thought without thinking') – are I think once again inconclusive. The first is inconclusive because that the distinction *may be* educationally unhelpful is well short of *is* or *must be* unhelpful; the advocate of thinking skills is open, as earlier, to remain an advocate but either reject the accompanying distinction or accept it but take it on board and endeavour to avoid the possible unhelpful educational consequences. It is, moreover, unclear just how this distinction may be educationally unhelpful: what specifically is unhelpful about it? For example, does it really require a complete divorce of beliefs from actions? The second difficulty can be avoided in at least two ways: our advocate of thinking skills can point out that while many skills (e.g., bicycle riding) typically do not involve thinking, thinking skills, unlike the others, do; or that just as bicycle riding doesn't require thinking about riding, exercising one's thinking skills (e.g., while solving a maths problem) doesn't require thinking about that exercise, but only about the mathematics involved in the problem about which one is thinking. While there is clearly much more that can be said here, the objections do seem inconclusive as they stand.

(iv) Johnson worries about the 'baleful influence' (p. 11) of focusing on sequentially and hierarchically organized sub-skills that might be encouraged by thinking of thinking as a skill. For one thing, such an approach 'does not even apply to many model cases of skill, such as crafts and sports' – his example here is David Beckham, who 'doesn't go through a checklist covering positioning of feet, body angle, follow through and the like in order to centre the ball. If he did, he wouldn't be David Beckham'. More generally, 'physical and practical skills of any complexity cannot be adequately taught by breaking each skill down into components: teaching "parts" is no guarantee that the learner acquires the whole' (p. 11). For another, teaching rules and principles governing the execution of skills is not necessary for student acquisition of the skill, and may often be educationally counterproductive: bicycle riding may depend upon the laws of physics, but it would be a pedagogical mistake to teach children to ride their bikes by teaching them the relevant physics and encouraging them to apply that understanding of physics to their cycling.

Both these points are worthwhile, although their bearing on the teaching of thinking skills is unclear, just because it is so far unclear how similar thinking skills (if there are such) are to crafts and sports skills like those involved in football playing and bicycle riding. While I won't dwell on this point, it does seem possible for the advocate of thinking skills to avoid these worries simply by distinguishing between thinking skills and other sorts of skills. And I should note that these worries don't seem to challenge the existence of thinking skills as such, but rather the wisdom of particular ways of teaching for them.

(v) The apparent dissimilarity between thinking skills and other sorts of skills just mentioned motivates Johnson's next objection: that unlike the skills of carpenters and gardeners, those of thinkers cannot be learned by observation and modelling (p. 12). This is not just because our thoughts are private; it is also because mental processes (if there are such) are not uniform and consistent in the way that, say, processes of joining and planting might be. Johnson uses the example of memory: 'there is no mental process of remembering common to all acts of memory' (pp. 12–13). Here the target of critique is not thinking of thinking as a skill, but rather thinking of thinking as composed of mental processes. We take up the question of mental processes below. Here I would point out just that remembering seems less apt an example than purported thinking skills or mental processes such as analysing or hypothesizing.

(vi) Johnson also objects to the idea, promulgated by both the McGuinness Report and thinkers such as Edward de Bono, that thinking is a skill that can be improved by practice. Here the worry is that while practice 'seems appropriate in the case of a skill where one can decide to exercise the skill and then monitor and control it with respect to a known end-product' (p. 13), that appropriateness is problematic when applied to thinking because (a) 'in the area of the intellect' it is not obvious that one can decide to do this: 'one cannot choose to understand something – we can neither initiate nor control it,' and (b) 'thinking will often not have a known end-product; it will often lead to more questions or deeper perplexity' (p. 13). As earlier, both points have merit, but their ability to challenge the idea that thinking is a skill is limited. The first is a correct point about understanding, but is not obviously correct when made about thinking, since we do seem able to choose to initiate thinking ('OK, my break is over; time to start thinking again about Johnson's critique of thinking skills.'). The second is also correct, but it is unclear why the open-endedness of some thinking counts as a reason for thinking that thinking can't or won't be improved by practice. (Student: 'After working hard on my philosophy course this term, I seem to be better at identifying, analysing and evaluating arguments, and at coming up with telling counter-examples, than I was at the start of term. My ability to think philosophically has been improved by lots of practice at philosophical thinking.') So again, Johnson's critical points, though correct, seem inconclusive.

What is the upshot of these several points? I think that many of Johnson's critical points are correct, but I'm less sure of their force as criticisms of the idea that thinking is rightly thought of in terms of skill. Johnson is clearly right that thinking is in several crucial respects quite unlike the skills involved in footballing, bicycling, carpentry, gardening and the like. Does this mean that thinking is not a skilled activity, or that thinking, if a skill, must be (for example) unthinking, etc.? These consequences do not seem to follow. Moreover, there is a more expansive understanding of thinking skills, according to which they are best seen not as unthinking processes, but rather as *abilities that admit of normative evaluation* (Bailin 1998, Bailin et. al. 1999, Bailin and Siegel 2003). Johnson and I are in the main agreed that thinking skills cannot be plausibly understood as particular 'private' mental processes or 'inner' entities. We are also agreed that it makes good sense to speak of thinking skills adverbially and adjectivally, as indicating thinking that is skilful in that it meets relevant criteria governing quality. The untoward associations between 'skills' and both unthinking habitual behaviours/mindless routines and untenable private mental processes can be severed, I think and hope, by speaking not of skills but of *abilities*, where such abilities are measures of the *quality* of a thinker's thinking. But in the end, whether we use the word 'skills' or the word 'abilities', the important point – on which Johnson and I are agreed – is that it is the quality of thinking that matters, and that when speaking of a thinker's thinking skills/abilities, we are referring not to any dubious private mental entities or processes, or unthinking habitual behaviours or mindless routines, but rather to the quality – the skilfulness – of that thinking, that is, the degree to which it meets relevant criteria (Bailin and Siegel 2003, p. 183).

Suppose for a moment that the case for this alternative conception of thinking skills can be compellingly made. Would this mean that Johnson's critique of the conception of thinking skills advanced in the McGuinness Report fails? Not at all. I think that Johnson's critique of that conception is powerfully made and in important respects completely telling. I am happy to join with Johnson in rejecting it. Nevertheless, I hope that the alternative conception of thinking skills just mentioned both makes philosophical sense and holds educational promise.

3. 'The myth of general transferability'

Are thinking skills generalizable or generally transferable? Johnson suggests not just that the McGuinness Report answers in the affirmative, but moreover that '[m]uch of the educational appeal of thinking skills stems from a mistaken belief in their general transferability' (p. 13), so that by undermining their transferability, the educational appeal of thinking skills will wane. What, exactly, does 'transferability' come to here? Johnson explicates it (in part) in terms of 'domain independence': a skill is generally transferable if its execution is independent of the domain in which it is executed (p. 14).

Are there any such generally transferable, domain independent skills? Consider the skills (if indeed these are rightly thought of as 'skills') of addition and the calculation of probabilities. Both of these 'belong' to specific domains, namely arithmetic and statistics/probability theory. But once acquired, they seem to be domain independent in that they can be exercised in a wide range of domains: If James can add, he can add not only in arithmetic class, but also in biology and English literature class, and also in the supermarket and while watching Beckham bend another one into the net and adding it to his running total of 'Beckham's benders'. Similarly, once Maria can calculate probabilities, she can do so not just in statistics class but also in her genetics and chemistry classes, when considering the likelihood and practical implications of weather conditions while planning her next driving holiday, and contemplating whether to vote Liberal in the next by-election or the wisdom of buying a lottery ticket in the upcoming drawing. Or consider the ability to detect a traditional fallacy like *post hoc ergo propter hoc* ('after this, therefore because of this'). Many advocates of critical thinking, myself included, have claimed that this ability is general or domain independent in that once mastered in a critical thinking class or elsewhere, it can be exercised in any domain in which the fallacy is manifested: in physics or history class, but also in assessing a proposed explanation of a surprising event, the reliability of the brand of car one is contemplating buying, the wisdom of the candidate one is contemplating supporting, or the worthiness of the candidate's party's platform. These examples seem enough to establish the prima facie plausibility of the claim that some skills are generalizable, transferable and domain independent: they can be applied, exercised, and manifested in many diverse situations and with respect to many diverse subject matters.

If they are indeed transferable, it is easy to understand why educators would want to focus on them: they would hope for a big pedagogical 'bang for the buck', since once taught such skills and abilities can be exercised in a broad range of domains, both in and beyond traditional school subjects. This is no doubt the explanation of McGuinness' and Scriven's praise (cited by Johnson, p. 14) of teaching such generalizable and transferable skills where one can.

Johnson argues that '[t]he idea of transfer itself is far more problematic than is generally recognized' (p. 14). What are his reasons for thinking it problematic? He gives several:

i. *Domain-Specific Content:* Although this reason is not developed in detail here, it is I think at the heart of Johnson's rejection of 'general transferability'. His view is that what appear to be general skills are actually domain-specific, and in two ways: they depend upon domain-specific content knowledge (so that, for example, my ability to identify an unstated assumption in an argument in the domain of chemistry depends upon my knowledge of chemistry); and, in addition, the ability itself is domain-specific in that if I have the ability to identify unstated assumptions of arguments in distinct domains, for example chemistry and aesthetics, they are actually two different skills/abilities: that of identifying the unstated assumptions of arguments in chemistry, and that of identifying such assumptions in arguments in aesthetics. In short, and in a slogan: *different domains; different skills*. As we proceed through the consideration of Johnson's more explicit reasons for doubting the existence of generally transferable skills next, these two reasons – that the exercise of skills depends upon domain-specific content knowledge; and that, when what is apparently the same skill is exercised in two or more different domains, it is, contrary to appearances, two or more different skills that are exercised – will be central to the discussion.

ii. *Similarity:* 'Transfer depends not only on there being an appropriate similarity between contexts, but also on this similarity being perceived by the person transferring the skill' (p. 14). I am inclined to agree with Johnson on this point, although I am unsure how self-conscious the perception in question need be. But it is unclear how damaging this point is to the 'general transferability' case, because it is unclear that any more is required than a recognition by the thinker that the contexts in question are such that the skills of addition, calculation of probabilities or identification of particular fallacies can be applied in each of them.

Johnson correctly notes both important philosophical difficulties, in particular those associated with Wittgenstein's and Kripke's worries about rule-following, and a depressing lack of evidence from psychology for the existence of generalizable, transferable skills (pp. 14–16). Despite these difficulties, belief in the existence of such skills, at least among some scholars, persists. As Johnson aptly puts it, such skills are, for many, 'simply too good not to be true' (p. 16). He also reviews three psychological theories that allegedly lend support to the existence of general transferable thinking skills – 'faculty psychology', 'identical elements' and 'information processing' (pp. 16–19) – and concludes that they offer no such support. He suggests that resistance to the case against generalizable, transferable skills results from conceptual errors, to which we turn next.

iii. *Conceptual Errors:* Johnson identifies several 'conceptual errors' that give illicit support to 'the myth of the general transferability of thinking skills' (p. 20): reification, essentialism, the naming fallacy, and the generalizing fallacy. Let us consider them in turn:

   a. *Reification:* Johnson defines reification as 'the act of wrongly treating X as if it were a *thing*. There might, however, be nothing wrong with treating lots of things as things, but it is important to treat them as the right sorts of things. One example of this error that is germane to our present inquiry is that, although we can refer to "thinking", there is no such thing as "thinking" *tout court*. This is because "think" takes an indirect object' (p. 20, emphases in original).

It is hard for me to believe that the last, grammatical point could be dispositive of the metaphysical question. It is also worth noting that treating thinking as the wrong sort of thing seems nevertheless to treat it as a thing, that is, as something that exists. But Johnson's most important claim here is that it is also an instance of objectionable reification to move 'from the properly adverbial or adjectival to the improperly substantive. It is often assumed that if X can do Y skilfully, there must be a skill of Y-ing and that X has it. For example, because it is meaningful to talk of someone who thinks well as being a skilful thinker, we are tempted to believe that there is a "skill" to be identified, isolated and trained for. Thus there is in effect a jump from talk of performing an action well or successfully to the existence of some specific, discrete skill or skills possessed by and exercised by the performer . . .' (p. 20).

This is an important point: To take our earlier examples, that Maggie can add numbers, calculate probabilities and identify particular fallacies skilfully does not entitle us to infer the existence of discrete 'skills' of addition, probability calculation and fallacy identification that can be 'identified, isolated and trained for'. Is Johnson right about this?

He may well be. But notice what has been built into the issue here: Johnson's objection turns out not to involve the positing or illicitly inferring of a non-existent skill, but rather the inferring of skills that can be 'identified, isolated and trained for'. Suppose he is right that, as a matter of fact, such skills cannot be 'isolated' from other related skills (e.g., addition from subtraction, calculating probabilities from multiplication, or identifying particular fallacies from identifying valid forms of reasoning) or 'trained for' in isolation from those other related skills. This would not touch the metaphysical issue of the skills' existence, but rather the pedagogical one of developing them in students effectively and efficiently.

Moreover, so understood the point at issue seems a straightforwardly empirical one: how 'isolatable' and 'trainable' are the skills in question? This does not seem to be the sort of issue that can be settled by armchair analysis.

Despite the worries just expressed, however, I am happy to side with Johnson here, at least for the sake of argument, because we are agreed on the fundamental point that these so-called skills are understood most importantly to be adverbial or adjectival descriptors of desirable student thinking. What we want, as educators, is to help students to think *well*: for example, to add (and subtract), calculate probabilities (and multiply) and identify fallacies (and valid forms of reasoning) skilfully. If we are agreed that that is our educational goal as far as thinking is concerned, the metaphysical question seems less pressing than Johnson's discussion suggests.

b. *Essentialism:* 'Essentialists in this area believe that just as acid has the power to turn litmus red or a magnet has the power to attract iron filings because of some underlying structures, so the ability to solve problems or to think critically is explicable in terms of underlying structures of the mind or brain' (p. 21). Johnson here cites Stephen Norris to this effect, and objects that 'transferring this idea from inorganic substances to human intellectual abilities can have unfortunate results. It may lead to motivation, beliefs, desires and context being ignored. Furthermore, general labels such as "problem-solving" or "critical thinking" gain a spurious unity and precision. Finally, this idea makes it difficult to explain how someone with the mental power of critical thinking could ever fail to think critically . . .' (p. 21).

These objections seem to me inconclusive. Taking the three critical points in order: First, that the positing of underlying structures *may* lead to the ignoring of motivation, beliefs, desires and context manifestly does not mean or entail that they *must* or *will in fact* be ignored in particular cases. Second, it is not clear why saying that James has the skill of (for example) identifying unstated assumptions and explaining this in terms of 'underlying structures of the mind or brain' imparts 'a spurious unity and precision', any more than saying that James 'identifies unstated assumptions skillfully' – a locution that Johnson allows – and explaining this in the same way imparts a spurious unity and precision. The final worry concerning explanation seems straightforwardly handled by distinguishing between the skill/ability to identify unstated assumptions and the having of the 'critical spirit', that is, the attitudes, dispositions, habit of mind and character traits inclining the thinker in question actually to do so (Siegel 1988). While I don't want to either commit myself to or defend 'essentialism' about thinking skills here, I don't see that Johnson's brief remarks undermine it.

c. *The Naming Fallacy:* Johnson says that '[t]his fallacy is committed by supposing the existence of a general skill or ability X, from the existence of a general label or category, X. In other words, because we have a general name which can be correctly applied to a range of activities, then it is assumed that there must be a general skill corresponding to that general name' (pp. 21–22). Johnson continues: 'I believe this fallacy may play a role in some defences of general thinking skills' (p. 28), singling out my own allegedly fallacious defence: 'Siegel says that a conception of thinking "must be possible, on pain of inability to identify all specific acts as acts of thinking"' (p. 22, citing Siegel 1990, p. 77; 'of thinking' italicized in the original). Being thus placed on the hook, I next defend myself from the charge that my arguments commit the 'naming fallacy'.

My defence is simple and straightforward: the quoted passage asserts that a 'conception of thinking' must be possible; it says nothing about any 'general skill' of thinking. My defence of general skills and abilities does not rest on any 'naming fallacy'; rather, it rests on (a) a critique of John McPeck's argument for his claim that teaching critical thinking is impossible on conceptual grounds, and (b) a straightforward empirical claim concerning what we routinely do:

> It makes perfect sense . . . to claim that one teaches CT [critical thinking], *simpliciter*, when one means that one helps students to

> develop reasoning skills which are general in that they can be applied to many diverse situations and subject matters . . . This point is supported, moreover, by the fact that there are readily identifiable reasoning skills which do not refer to any specific subject matter, which do apply to diverse situations, and which are in fact the sort of skill which courses in CT seek to develop. Skills such as identifying assumptions, tracing relationships between premises and conclusions, identifying standard fallacies, and so on, do not require the identification of specific subject matters: such skills are germane to thinking in subject areas as diverse as physics, religion, and photography. (Siegel 1990, p. 77)

This passage was originally published more than twenty years ago, and if I were writing it anew I would no doubt write it somewhat differently. In particular, I would clarify my use of 'skill' and its relation to the less disputed word 'ability', as I have in more recent publications (and briefly above). Nevertheless, it is apparent that there is no 'naming fallacy' here – I did not argue from 'there is a general category, "thinking",' to 'there is a general skill of thinking.'

However, I did argue that there is a legitimate general category, 'thinking', and that there must therefore be *some* possible conception of thinking insofar as we are able to identify particular specific acts as acts *of thinking*. Is *this* an instance of the 'naming fallacy'? Whether or not Johnson thinks so, his text makes clear that there is in his view *something* wrong with this argument, and he cites Ryle and Wittgenstein in his defence (p. 22). But I am unmoved by the appeal to these two eminences, and reject the latter's famous 'family resemblance' account of particular concepts like that of 'game' in favour of Bernard Suits' analysis of the latter in his brilliant but little-known *The Grasshopper*. (Suits 2005; thanks to Colin McGinn for bringing Suits' book to my attention.) Johnson suggests that 'if Ryle or Wittgenstein is right then those arguing for general thinking skills on the basis that all examples of thinking have common features would have a problem' (p. 22). But that they do have many things in common is incontrovertible: they all count as examples of thinking; they all count as mental acts or events of one sort or another; they all depend on or are manifestations of particular sorts of brain activity; etc. The question before us is not whether they have anything in common, which they undeniably do, but rather: do such commonalities provide a basis for thinking that there are general thinking skills, and did I argue for the latter on that basis? I agree with Johnson that the inference is problematic. But it is simply false that I drew this inference, or appealed to any such argument. One needn't – and I didn't – argue for the existence of general thinking skills 'on the basis that all examples of thinking have common features'. In my earlier discussion, cited above, my first point was aimed at McPeck's conceptual argument against the very coherence of (teaching for) general skills of critical thinking. I then argued for the existence of such skills on the rather more straightforward basis of pointing to the sort of teaching many of us do everyday in our introductory philosophy/informal logic/critical thinking courses. ('*Assignment*: Read the following passages, taken from texts originally appearing in philosophy, psychology, history, literature, biology and physics textbooks or journals, as well as from novels and other literary works, popular magazines and newspaper editorials. For each, identify unstated assumptions, reconstruct arguments in premise-conclusion form, state the nature of the relationship between the premises and conclusions, and evaluate the arguments, identifying any particular fallacies.') That we do this suggests that there is something mistaken about McPeck's claim that it is impossible to do so, and with Johnson's suggestion that doing so requires committing the 'naming fallacy'. And indeed Johnson's several criticisms of my view (pp. 22–24) do not attend to, or even mention, the actual argument given in the passage cited above and just rehearsed – that is, the argument by example, that there are *in fact* some thinking skills that are general in the sense that they can be applied to many diverse situations and subject matters – and *here are some of them*. Teachers of critical thinking courses endeavour to foster the development of skills in their students that 'are general in that they can be applied to many diverse situations and subject matters ... [T]here are readily identifiable reasoning skills which do not refer to any specific subject matter, which do apply to diverse situations, and which are in fact the sort of skill which courses in critical thinking seek to develop. Skills such as identifying assumptions, tracing relationships between premises and conclusions, identifying standard fallacies, and so on' (Siegel 1990, p. 77) are not only in principle teachable, *contra* McPeck; they are actually taught in some successful critical thinking courses, and so indeed exist, *contra* Johnson. (For empirical evidence on this, see the references to some empirical literature in Siegel (2008, p. 177). For discussion of McPeck's claim that such alleged skills as identifying assumptions are themselves subject-specific, see Siegel (1988, pp. 20–21), and below.)

Johnson challenges the analogy I drew between thinking and cycling – again, an analogy drawn in the course of challenging McPeck's claim that because specific acts of thinking are always acts of thinking *about something*, general thinking skills are on conceptual grounds impossible and so necessarily non-existent. Here's what I wrote back then:

> It is not the case that the general activity of thinking is 'logically connected to an X,' any more than the general activity of cycling is logically connected to any particular bicycle. It is true that any given act of cycling must be done on some bicycle or other. But it surely does not follow that the general activity of cycling cannot be discussed independently of any particular bicycle. Indeed, we can state, and teach people, general skills of cycling (e.g., 'Lean to the left when making a left-hand turn,' 'Slow down before cornering, not during cornering,' etc.), even though instantiating these maneuvers and so exhibiting mastery of the general skills requires some particular bicycle . . . As with cycling, so with thinking. Thus, McPeck's suggestion that teaching CT *simpliciter* is a conceptual impossibility is mistaken. As we can teach cycling, so we can teach CT. (Siegel 1990, p. 77)

Johnson objects to the analogy between cycling and thinking, as follows: 'This, however, is not very convincing, partly for the reasons given earlier for not regarding thinking as a skill, and partly because cycling is, in fact, a very specific activity rather than a general one, with an obvious and limited set of standards and criteria of effectiveness. Moreover, bicycles seem much more alike than, for instance, areas of critical thought such as chemistry and aesthetics' (p. 23).

None of these three reasons are compelling. The first, involving Johnson's 'reasons given earlier for not regarding thinking as a skill', is not compelling because those reasons are, as suggested above, at best inconclusive.

The second reason, that 'cycling is, in fact, a very specific activity rather than a general one', betokens an important potential ambiguity. In the earlier citation above, it is clear that when speaking of 'general thinking skills' I did not suggest that 'thinking' is itself one general skill, but rather that particular reasoning skills 'are general in that they can be applied to many diverse situations and subject matters'; and in the most recently cited passage I offer as examples the specific reasoning skills of 'identifying assumptions, tracing relationships between premises and conclusions, [and] identifying standard fallacies'. My claim was and is that such skills as these are indeed 'general' in the sense specified: once acquired, they can be applied, exercised and manifested in many diverse situations and with respect to diverse subject matters. Students can, for example, become skilled at identifying unstated assumptions, and exercise that ability in quite diverse contexts. Does Johnson really doubt this? Indeed, I'd wager that he has honed the skill to a considerable degree himself, and would do very well indeed on the parenthetical, hypothetical 'assignment' mentioned above. Johnson's explication of 'general' in terms of 'general transferability' mentioned above – that is, that a skill is generally transferable if the execution of it is independent of the domain in which it is executed – seems to make his use of the term more or less equivalent to mine. If so, my examples of general skills seem to qualify as generally transferable skills in Johnson's sense. If so, these general skills are 'general' in just the relevant sense – as are the general skills involved in cycling, for example, regulating one's speed properly before and during cornering.

Johnson's third reason, that bicycles seem more alike than 'areas of critical thought such as chemistry and aesthetics', unfairly switches from a claim about skills to a claim about 'areas'. No one has suggested that chemistry is relevantly like aesthetics. The claim, rather, is that (for example) identifying unstated assumptions of arguments, identifying patterns of reasoning in such arguments, and/or judging the epistemic quality of such arguments, are relevantly similar in the two areas. Johnson has provided no reason for doubting this – although we will have to face the objection (made by McPeck 1990, pp. 96–7 and elsewhere) that these seemingly general skills/abilities are in fact not general, but rather 'domain specific', not just because their proper exercise in any given domain depends upon domain-specific knowledge, but because the skills/abilities themselves differ from domain to domain, so that (for example) the ability to identify unstated assumptions of arguments in the domain of chemistry is a different ability than the ability to identify unstated assumptions of arguments in the domain of aesthetics. Indeed, I suspect that Johnson might balk at my attempt to merge our respective senses of 'general', and urge that, for example, the ability to identify unstated assumptions is *not* such that its execution is 'independent of the domain in which it is executed'. Rather, if my suspicion is correct, that ability is on Johnson's view 'domain relative': not only might a given student successfully identify unstated assumptions of arguments in one domain (e.g., chemistry) but fail to do so in another (for example, aesthetics); more importantly, when that student successfully identifies unstated assumptions in the two domains, she is executing two distinct, domain-relative skills: identifying unstated assumptions of arguments in chemistry, and identifying unstated assumptions of arguments in aesthetics. I concede immediately that Johnson nowhere asserts this in his text, and my suspicion may well be mistaken. But whether or not Johnson makes this move, McPeck certainly does:

> Take . . . 'the ability to recognize underlying assumptions.' That this is not a singular ability can be appreciated by considering the fact that to recognize an underlying assumption in mathematics requires a different set of skills and abilities from those required for recognizing them in a political dispute, which are different again from those required in a scientific dispute. Thus, the phrase 'ability to recognize underlying assumptions' does not denote any singular uniform ability, but rather a wide variety of them. (McPeck 1990, p. 97)

And so I should next say a word about it.

In fact there is much to say here, in particular concerning the role of *domain-specific knowledge* in the exercise of such skills as that of identifying unstated assumptions. Surely one reason that a student might successfully identify the unstated assumptions of arguments in chemistry but fail to do so in arguments in aesthetics is her knowledge of chemistry and her lack of knowledge of aesthetics. I agree with both Johnson and McPeck that subject- or domain-specific knowledge is often required for the successful execution of a given skill/ability in a given domain. But is McPeck right that these are different abilities, or, as he puts it in the passage just cited, that each 'requires a different set of skills and abilities'? I see no reason to think so. Just as my ability to ride a bicycle is not relative to different bicycles, such that I have one ability to ride my new blue one, another to ride my old yellow one, and yet another to ride your green one – it's all one ability, exercised on different bicycles – Steve's ability to identify unstated assumptions is not one ability when exercised on argument A from chemistry, another when exercised on argument B from aesthetics, and yet another when exercised on argument C from the editorial pages concerning some current political matter. Even though Steve's execution of his ability to identify unstated assumptions in these different domains might depend upon his domain-specific knowledge, it is nevertheless one ability, exercised in different domains and perhaps utilizing different domain-specific information. (I leave aside the difficult matter of the individuation of 'domains'. Suppose Steve can identify the unstated assumptions of arguments in organic chemistry, but not in quantum chemistry. Do these then count as distinct domain-specific abilities? How would one stop the unwelcome result that the identification of every unstated assumption amounts to a distinct ability? Is it a different ability every time an unstated assumption is identified in an argument – that is, is this ability not just domain-relative but *argument*-relative? Should we say similar things about addition: the ability to add one pair of numbers is one ability, and to add another pair another? Is reading words with four letters a different ability than reading words with five? This seems very bad news for teachers of arithmetic and reading, and is contrary to Johnson's rejection of the idea that skills are composed of component micro-skills.) The alternative seems to lead inexorably to a vast multiplication of skills/abilities, which seems both contrary to ordinary language and ordinary thinking ('he's a skilled driver'; 'she's very good at identifying unstated assumptions'; 'he's a poor reader'; etc.) and troublesome pedagogically.

I do not see in Johnson's discussion (or McPeck's) any good reason to regard skills/abilities such as those of identifying unstated assumptions, putting arguments in premise-conclusion form, and our other examples, as domain- or argument-relative. Rather, we should regard them as general, in the sense specified above. This is completely compatible with the point that their successful execution is often dependent on domain-specific knowledge. Even if Johnson is right to insist that, for example, the successful execution of Maggie's skill at identifying unstated assumptions is domain-relative, in that Maggie is better at identifying such assumptions in chemistry than she is in aesthetics (perhaps in part because of her knowledge of chemistry), it remains nonetheless both that the skill is separable from the knowledge, at least conceptually; and, more importantly for present purposes, that the execution of the skill in chemistry, even if dependent on knowledge of chemistry, is not thereby a different skill from that of identifying unstated assumptions in aesthetics.

It is also worth mentioning Ennis' 'infusion' approach to the teaching of critical thinking, in which principles of critical thinking are taught, and skills developed, by explicitly discussing the principles in the context of the treatment of subject matter content (Ennis 1989, 1996). Ennis' approach clearly integrates general skills/abilities and domain-specific content in a way that raises doubts about Johnson's rejection of general, transferable skills.

I conclude that the 'naming fallacy' is a red herring. For one thing, my earlier discussion does not manifest the allegedly fallacious pattern of reasoning. For another, the passages Johnson focuses on in his critique are aimed not at establishing the existence of general thinking skills, but rather at undermining McPeck's linguistic/conceptual arguments for the *a priori* impossibility of the existence of such skills and of teaching for them. More importantly, the argument for the existence of general reasoning skills does not rest on linguistic or grammatical or conceptual points, but rather on the obvious (and empirically measurable and measured) existence of specific such skills.

d. *The Generalizing Fallacy:* 'This error consists in putting a task competence under the heading of a wider, perhaps an extremely wide, task descriptor and assuming that if a person has mastered the task competence then, *ipso facto*, she can do whatever falls under the wider descriptor' (p. 30). Johnson's examples, for example, of generalizing from 'Martin knows how to use a tin opener' to 'Martin knows how to use (all) tools,' and from 'Martin can use a kitchen knife' to 'Martin can perform brain surgery' are telling; these would clearly be unjustified generalizations. To the extent that the McGuinness report and other official documents commit this fallacy, I am happy to join with Johnson in condemning it. That said, however, the extent to which it is committed in such documents is unclear. Johnson writes: '[T]he theory that relies on the existence of general strategies proposes that there is such a thing as, for example, problem-solving *simpliciter* . . . Thus there *could appear to be* some transfer between finding what is wrong with an inoperative washing machine and spotting the flaw in an invalid syllogism' (p. 25, last emphasis added). Taking this passage at face value, Johnson does not claim that the report asserts that there is in fact any such transfer. Where, then, is the fallacy? In any case, if the fallacy is indeed committed, I'm happy to join in Johnson's condemnation of it.

There seems to be a degree of talking-past-one-another here, again involving what counts as 'general'. My own view is that various skills, abilities and dispositions of critical thinking are general in that once acquired, they can be applied, exercised and manifested in many diverse situations and contexts, with respect to many diverse subject matters. These include skills/abilities such as identifying assumptions and reconstructing arguments in premise-conclusion form, and dispositions such as demanding reasons for and seeking counter-examples to specific assertions or claims (Siegel 1988, 1997, ch. 2). These claims of mine seem to me to be innocent of what Johnson calls the 'generalising fallacy'. But Johnson might judge them guilty, on grounds that identifying assumptions and seeking counter-examples in one domain are different from identifying assumptions and seeking counter-examples in other domains. If so, the matter has already been addressed in the previous section's discussion of domain-specific content knowledge.

4. The 'direct' teaching of thinking and content/subject matter knowledge

Are there 'free-floating', subject-independent thinking skills, that is, skills that are not tied to any particular subject, domain, or content area? If so, should they be taught 'directly'? (p. 25) Johnson challenges the latter idea that skills can be taught 'directly'; his challenge rests heavily on challenging the free-floatingness or subject-independence of such skills.

i. Can/should thinking skills be taught 'directly'?

It is somewhat unclear what Johnson means by the 'direct' teaching of thinking skills; as far as I can tell he means to reject the idea that such skills can be taught 'explicitly', without reference to any subject matter content or independently of all context (pp. 26–27). Johnson is clear that his main objection to the 'direct' approach to teaching thinking is its 'devaluing of knowledge', and he amasses an impressive series of quotations from several authors, including McGuinness, to the effect that 'knowledge gets in the way' of the effective teaching of thinking skills (p. 27). Johnson advocates a 'conception of thinking . . . that is sensitive to and energized by detailed content', and suggests that 'appropriate, detailed, subject-specific knowledge renders thinking skills redundant' (p. 27). He illustrates his view by considering 'the popular general thinking skill of "comparing"', pointing out that comparing requires 'appropriate knowledge of what is to be compared, awareness of the appropriate frame of reference and awareness of the appropriate criteria . . . [as well as] the need for motivation to carry out the comparison'. His objection is straightforward: 'These three epistemic requirements are likely to be so specific as to have little or no relevance to many other comparisons that one wishes to make. Moreover, given that someone has the motivation, identifies the frame of reference, knows what criteria are relevant and has the appropriate knowledge, what sense could be made of them stating that they cannot make the comparison because they lack the skill? In fact, there is no work for the supposed skill of comparing to do' (pp. 27–28).

I have no wish to defend the existence of a general thinking skill of 'comparing', or to defend a 'direct' method of teaching it. But it does seem to me that Johnson's earlier acceptance of the idea that we can think more or less skilfully undermines his argument here. Advocates of the general skill would no doubt reply to Johnson that the work the supposed skill of comparing would do, if possessed, is that of enabling thinkers to compare more skilfully than they would if they lacked the skill, or possessed it to a lesser degree. It certainly seems possible for a thinker to have the motivation and meet the epistemic requirements Johnson sets out, and yet carry out the comparison badly, ineptly, or simply not maximally well (just as a carpenter may have the motivation and meet the analogues of Johnson's epistemic requirements, yet lack the skill and so fail to make an excellent dovetail joint). If so, there does seem to be work for the supposed skill to do. As already noted, I have no wish to join the issue with Johnson over the example of 'comparing'. But I would take issue with other skills, such as those essential to critical thinking that I've been using as running examples throughout (identifying unstated assumptions and valid/ fallacious patterns of reasoning, assessing the epistemic merits of arguments, etc.). Here Johnson's claim that knowledge is all seems to me not just implausible but false, since it is very common for teachers of critical thinking to have experience of students who have the relevant knowledge but lack the skill (e.g., of identifying unstated assumptions), and the quality of whose thinking suffers as a result.

I should also note that the 'content knowledge vs. skill' dichotomy that Johnson's argument here presupposes is itself problematic. As William Hare has definitively established, advocates of critical thinking do not in general reject subject matter content knowledge; rather, they see skills and knowledge as working together in the development and exercise of the relevant skills and abilities (Hare 1995; cf. the compelling examples and discussion in Scheffler 1989). If by rejecting the 'direct' teaching of thinking skills Johnson means to reject the idea that such skills can be taught without reference to any subject matter content whatsoever, or independently of all context, I happily join him in rejecting it – on this point he'll find few philosophers who would disagree. To teach students to identify unstated assumptions, for example, one has to work with examples of arguments containing unstated assumptions, and those examples will of course have some content or other. Nevertheless, once students have acquired some ability to identify unstated assumptions, that ability is not limited to the content or context utilized in first acquiring the ability – it can in principle, and typically in practice, be applied, exercised and manifested in many diverse situations and subject matters.

ii. Are thinking skills subject-independent?

If there is indeed 'work for the supposed skill to do', what should we say of the subject-independence of such skills? My own view, as already indicated, is that some such skills – for example, those of identifying unstated assumptions, or spotting fallacies such as *post hoc ergo propter hoc* – are independent of specific subjects in that the skills, once acquired, can be applied, exercised and manifested in many diverse situations and with respect to many diverse subject matters. For example, Matilda might be very good at identifying unstated assumptions, detecting them easily in textbooks, newspaper articles, and so on, while Matthew might be less good at it.

5. Mental processes and general thinking skills

Is thinking rightly thought of in terms of *mental processes*? Johnson doesn't exactly deny the existence of such processes, though he is clearly doubtful of their existence, calling such processes 'probably illusory' (p. 28). But he is very clearly concerned about pedagogical calamities that might flow from thinking of thinking in terms of such processes. Consider, for example, the supposed process of 'analysis'. Whether or not this is a genuine process, thinking that it is runs the risk of committing the naming fallacy, with predictable bad ramifications for teaching and learning: 'whether we are engaged in chemical analysis or we are analysing a poem, or a chess problem, it may be thought that we are engaged in *one and the same* process' (p. 29, emphasis in original). But these are clearly not instances of one and the same process. Thinking of thinking in terms of mental processes might also lead to thinking that 'thinking can be reduced to a set of pre-specified steps', thus leaving no room in our understanding of thinking for 'flashes of insight, leaps, jumps, speculation and the like that are part and parcel of human inquiry' (p. 29). Since thinking in terms of mental processes puts us at risk of making these mistakes, Johnson suggests, we should not think of thinking in those terms.

A further worry is the advice of advocates of thinking skills that learners should 'become aware of their own mental processes': As McGuinness puts it, 'developing thinking requires that children make their own thought processes more explicit thus enabling them to reflect upon their strategies' (p. 30; citation from DFEE, p. 5). Johnson objects that such processes, even if real, are not generally accessible through introspection; that experts do not exercise their expertise by reflecting upon and improving their strategies, but rather by utilizing vast repertoires of knowledge of typical cases and recognizing special cases; and that 'there are no rules or processes for having new ideas', for which 'imagination based on sound knowledge and understanding of the subject' is essential. He also emphasizes the importance for skilled thinking of several 'virtues, dispositions and circumstances', which again cannot be understood in terms of mental processes. He objects that even if the existence of mental processes is conceded, their relevance to the teaching of general thinking skills is doubtful (p. 44). Finally, Johnson challenges the identification, by psychologists and educationalists, of specific supposed general thinking skills, arguing in each case that their existence is dubious. He finds the supposed skills of distinguishing fact from opinion, observation, checking the reliability of evidence and being systematic, all problematic (pp. 34–36).

Details aside, I find Johnson's several criticisms of the pedagogical suggestions just mentioned which are alleged to flow from thinking of skills in terms of mental processes, and his criticisms of these particular supposed general thinking skills, on the whole plausible. (See also Bailin's (1998) criticism of thinking of thinking in terms of mental processes.) In any case, I have no wish to defend his targets here. (However, it seems to me that the point about encouraging students to reflect on their own thinking – which reflection is I think on the whole quite salutary – can be rendered in terms that don't require appeal to problematic processes, and that, so rendered, educators ought indeed to encourage students to so reflect.) So I move on to his final thesis, that '[t]he present preoccupation with thinking skills is educationally dangerous' (p. 36).

6. The educational dangers of thinking of thinking in terms of skills

Johnson considers four such dangers:

i. *Disparagement of Subject Knowledge:* 'There is a real danger that subject knowledge will be seen as nothing more than material on which to practice skills, or even as something that gets in the way of the real business of education: thinking skills' (p. 37).

I certainly agree with Johnson that knowledge is important, and if some advocates of thinking skills disparage it, I'm happy to join with him in condemning such disparagement and standing up for knowledge (Siegel 1998). But it is not the case that advocates of thinking skills cannot also acknowledge the importance of subject knowledge, as Johnson here intimates. As we've seen above, some advocates of thinking skills – especially those philosophers who advocate the importance of critical thinking, myself included – urge the importance of both. There is no contradiction in holding both that subject-specific knowledge is important, and that the mastery of skills and abilities which are general in that they can be applied, exercised and manifested in many diverse situations and subject matters is also important. So this danger seems to me avoidable, and I join with Johnson in urging its avoidance.

ii. *Thinking of Thinking as Impersonal and Value-Neutral:* Johnson here cites de Bono, who urges the production of a 'detached' thinking skill so that students/thinkers will be able to criticize their own thinking without feeling threatened; Johnson objects to such detachment on the grounds that 'Thinking is constitutive of our humanity and of who we are,' and is not detachable from our dispositions, personalities, virtues and moral and other values (p. 38). I quite agree with Johnson's claim about the connection between our thinking and the rest of us, but I'm not sure I quite grasp why he rejects de Bono's call for students to develop the ability to criticize their own thinking. Surely one can – and in my view should – acknowledge the 'undetachability' of thought from actions, values and the like while simultaneously plumping for the development of student ability to critically examine their own thinking. As above, the danger of concern to Johnson here is avoidable, and I join with him in urging its avoidance.

iii. *Lack of Enthusiasm for Truth:* Here we can be brief: Johnson is right that truth is important, right that we must not lose sight of it in our educational endeavours, and right that we need not do so. He happily does not claim that 'those who espouse thinking skills' must disparage truth, since they manifestly need not; I agree with Johnson that they should not (Siegel 1998).

iv. *The Computerisation of Thought:* 'Many of my misgivings about thinking skills', Johnson writes, 'may be summarized as worries about the computerization of thought. Cognitive psychologists like McGuinness tend to view the brain as a computer. Computers manipulate data according to rules; problems must be explicitly defined and broken down, and then procedures applied. This model of thought can lead to the illusion that all intelligent thinking is logical and rule-governed . . . Human thought and behaviour doesn't fit this model. Much of our thinking is intuitive and speculative. And even if some behaviour can be described *as if* it is rule-following, the proposed underlying rules play no part in the behaviour' (p. 41, emphasis in original). Johnson objects as well that the 'computer model of thought' requires the explicit defining of problems, the separation of thinkers from the world, and the replacement of imagination and creativity with the rule-governed exchange and manipulation of information, all of which Johnson regards as problematic (pp. 41–42).

I am sympathetic with several of Johnson's objections to the computer model of thought. (Several of the same points are made in Scheffler 1991.) I would note only that one can be an advocate of thinking skills without embracing the computer model. So again, as above, the dangers Johnson here points out can be avoided by such advocates.

7. Conclusion

It is in the nature of exercises like this one that criticism comes to the fore; the reader should therefore not be blamed if she comes away with the impression that my disagreements with Johnson are severe. In fact, they are not: we agree on much, and our disagreements, though not insignificant, should not obscure the large overlap in our views.

The main substantive disagreement between us is that concerning generalizability. For the reasons given above, I continue to hold that it makes perfect sense to think – despite Johnson's protestations – that some thinking skills/abilities are generalizable in that once acquired, they can be applied, exercised and manifested in many diverse situations/contexts and with respect to many diverse subject matters. It may well be that our apparent disagreement on this point stems in the end from disparate understandings of 'generalizability'. It is for that reason that I have tried to be clear about my own understanding of the term. If it turns out that Johnson's rejection of general thinking skills is based on a different understanding of it, our views will then turn out to be closer still.

The attentive reader will have noticed a recurring theme of my discussion: that Johnson's criticisms of thinking skills are often telling, but that advocates of thinking skills needn't embrace the objectionable targets of Johnson's critique. The key to avoiding them is resolutely to refrain from thinking of skills, including thinking skills, in terms of mysterious processes or habitual and mindless routines, and to insist on understanding skilled thinking in terms of *quality*: that is, as thinking that admits of positive normative evaluation in that it meets relevant criteria (Bailin and Siegel 2003).

Would this understanding of thinking skills be consistent with the McGuinness Report, the National Curriculum or the understanding of thinking skills promulgated by the British educational establishment? Here I am content to yield the floor to Johnson and the many others more familiar with the British educational scene than me. But I am happy to join with Johnson in condemning the untenable understanding of thinking skills he rightly criticizes, and in likewise condemning the many pedagogical sins he identifies, while upholding the importance of the fundamentally *normative* dimension of thinking, which is skilled exactly insofar as it is of a certain quality, that is, that satisfies relevant criteria to an appropriate degree.

References

Bailin, S. (1998), 'Education, knowledge and critical thinking', in D. Carr (ed.), *Education, Knowledge and Truth: Beyond the Postmodern Impasse*. London: Routledge, pp. 204–220.

Bailin, S., Case, R., Coombs, J. R. and Daniels, L. B. (1999), 'Conceptualizing critical thinking', *Journal of Curriculum Studies*, 31:3, 285–302.

Bailin, S. and H. Siegel (2003), 'Critical thinking', in N. Blake, P. Smeyers, R. Smith, and P. Standish (eds), *The Blackwell Guide to the Philosophy of Education*. Oxford: Blackwell, pp. 181–193.

DFEE, (1999), *From Thinking Skills to Thinking Classrooms*, London: HMSO.

Ennis, R. H. (1989), 'Critical thinking and subject specificity: Clarification and needed research', *Educational Researcher*, 18:3, 4–10.

—(1996), *Critical Thinking*, Upper Saddle River, NJ: Prentice-Hall.

Hare, W. (1995), 'Content and criticism: The aims of schooling', *Journal of Philosophy of Education*, 29:1, 47–60.

Johnson, S. (2010), 'Teaching Thinking Skills', this volume.

McPeck, J. E. (1990), *Teaching Critical Thinking*. New York: Routledge.

Scheffler, I. (1989), 'Moral education and the democratic ideal', reprinted in Scheffler, *Reason and Teaching*. Indianapolis: Hackett Publishing Company, pp. 136–145. Originally published by Routledge & Kegan Paul, 1973.

—(1991), 'Computers at schools?', reprinted in Scheffler, *In Praise of the Cognitive Emotions*. New York: Routledge, pp. 80–96. Originally published in *Teachers College Record*, 87:4 (1986): 513–28.

Siegel, H. (1988), *Educating Reason: Rationality, Critical Thinking, and Education*. London: Routledge.

—(1990), 'McPeck, informal logic and the nature of critical thinking', reprinted in J. E. McPeck, *Teaching Critical Thinking*, New York: Routledge, pp. 75–85. Originally published in *Philosophy of Education 1985: Proceedings of the Forty-First Annual Meeting of the Philosophy of Education Society*, Normal, IL: Philosophy of Education Society, pp. 61–72; also in Siegel 1988, ch. 1.

—(1997), *Rationality Redeemed?: Further Dialogues on an Educational Ideal*. New York: Routledge.

—(1998), 'Knowledge, truth and education', in D. Carr (ed.), *Education, Knowledge and Truth: Beyond the Postmodern Impasse*. London: Routledge, pp. 19–36.

—(2008), 'Autonomy, critical thinking and the Wittgensteinian legacy: Reflections on Christopher Winch, *Education, Autonomy and Critical Thinking*', *Journal of Philosophy of Education*, 42:1, 165–184.

Suits, B. (2005), *The Grasshopper: Games, Life and Utopia*. Peterborough, Canada: Broadview Press. Originally published by University of Toronto Press in 1978.

Further reading

For a recent overview, see also: Jan Sobocan and Leo Groarke, with Ralph H. Johnson and Frederick S. Ellett, Jr., (eds), *Critical Thinking Education and Assessment: Can Higher Order Thinking Be Tested?*, London, Ontario: The Althouse Press, 2009.

Afterword
Christopher Winch

> **Chapter Outline**
> 1. Skills — 88
> 2. Skills and transferability — 96
> 3. The question of efficacy — 101
> 4. What is thinking? — 103
> 5. Mental processes — 104
> 6. A summary of Johnson's claims — 107
> 7. Reasoning — 109
> 8. The role of philosophy — 112
> 9. Reason and argument — 113
> 10. Inductive arguments — 120
> 11. Concluding remarks — 122
>   References — 123

In this afterword, I attempt to follow up some of the issues raised in the debate between Johnson and Siegel. In doing so I attempt to clarify what I take to be some of the points of agreement, as well as of disagreement, between the two authors and also to follow up some considerations that were not perhaps considered to be too important by them but which have some further practical and philosophical interest, particularly in relation to our understanding of practical knowledge. The debate about thinking skills is concerned with the existence or otherwise of a particular kind of practical ability, call it a 'thinking skill' for the moment, although we shall see that this phrase has various problems associated with its use. Johnson identifies these supposed abilities as having the property of being 'generally transferable', a term with which Siegel does not dissent, although, unlike Johnson, he believes that such abilities do exist. The term implies that an ability being generally transferable means that it is *both* general in scope *and* transferable in application from one subject or context to another. However, abilities generally do not fall into the category of being either *generally transferable* or *particular and non-transferable* since it is evident that, for example, there are many highly specific skills that can, once learned in one context or in relation to one subject, be transferred to other contexts or subjects. It could be that all practical abilities that are general are also transferable, although that would have to be demonstrated case by case. We should also note that generality in this context is a relative term: ability A may be more general (in terms of the range of contexts in which it potentially has an application) than ability B, while ability C may be more general in this sense than either A or B.

However, thinking skills, if such there be, are not general in the sense that the ability of a carpenter is more general than the ability to saw wood. The former consists of a variety of other, more specific abilities combined, perhaps, with the ability to integrate various specific skills into the carrying out of particular projects, like the construction of tables. The carpenter may well be expected to plan, control, co-ordinate and evaluate his or her work and very often a successful carpenter will be someone who is said to be *thoughtful* about what he or she does. Indeed, one could plausibly claim that such a carpenter, to the extent that he or she plans, controls, co-ordinates and evaluates their work, demonstrates the ability to think about what they are doing and hence uses thinking skills.

The carpenter's work is thus general in the sense that it comprises a range of related abilities and skills which have to be brought together for the successful achievement of a project. However, the carpenter's work is also, arguably, general in another sense. If he or she is successful because they are thoughtful in their work then that is because such carpenters bring to bear on their work a range of abilities that, although they are embedded in the activities of a carpenter, can also be deployed in other kinds of activities. For example, the ability to plan ahead is not just a valued attribute of the occupational abilities of carpenters but also of sculptors, teachers and generals, to mention just a few. Since such abilities, once acquired, can be employed in a wide variety of activities, one might claim that to say that they are *transferable* is to say much the same thing as to say that they are general.

If, on the other hand, the ability to plan was specific to particular activities, so that the planning done by a carpenter was different from that done by a military strategist, one would wish to deny that planning was general ability, or at least affirm that its generality was restricted. *A fortiori* it would not be transferable from the activity of carpentry to that of military strategy. In these cases abilities which, when exercised, have the potential to occur within a wide range of other abilities, could be said to be general in a somewhat different sense to the first as they do, in a sense, *infuse* a range of abilities rather than merely being wide in their sphere of operations. The idea of general transferability/particular non-transferability might not then be applicable to every activity or every aspect of an activity, but it could be associated with abilities which could plausibly be said to be features of other abilities, perhaps features whose presence enhanced the quality of performance of the activities associated with those abilities.

But there is a further feature of such abilities which we need to note. It is not simply that they appear to have the potential to occur within the exercise of a range of other abilities but that they also appear to be incapable of being exercised *except* within the context of some particular activity. One cannot plan *tout court*, for example, one must plan something or other, one must be creative with respect to some medium or other, one must compare one or more things in *some respect* or other and so on. It seems then that the general transfer claim made in relation to thinking abilities has to be one that maintains that there is sufficient in the planning etc. in ability of type A to warrant our calling it the same ability when exercised in an ability of type B. It is not that thinking *could* be something done independently of any activity, and which just happened to be applicable to a range of different types of activities, but rather it is in the nature of a thinking ability it cannot but be applied to particular types of activity in order to be instantiated. So we can see that the claim that a thinking ability is general and that it is transferable stand or fall together, and that thinking abilities are by their nature implicated in other abilities. This makes them somewhat different from many of the other abilities that we are called on to develop and assess and this makes their treatment rather more complex.

1. Skills

First, it is necessary to consider the term 'skill'. In the English language, a *skill*, which is a form of practical knowledge or know-how, is conceptually linked to a type of *task*, such as firing a bow and arrow, forming a pot, cutting wood etc. So it appears as if a skill is a kind of ability to perform a task, typically, but by no means exclusively, a manual task. In fact, the issue is slightly more complicated by an ambiguity in our use of the term 'skill'. We often say that 'so and so has a skill', implying that the skill is a possession of that person. But it also makes sense to say that more than one person has the same skill. In this second sense, a skill is more like a *technique* or way of carrying out a type of task, which can then be learned and applied by individuals who may then become skilled in the exercise of that technique and hence acquire that skill as a personal attribute. A type of task that has varying ranges of applicability and the acquisition of a technique, such as that of sawing wood, usually means that the possessor of such a skill will be able to apply it in a range of situations, which is not precisely determinate. Few skills are applicable to only one task or one very narrowly defined type of task, although some highly specialized skills fall into this category. In this sense, all skills possess some degree of *generality*, although Siegel would distinguish this from *universality*, which would imply that a skill could be applied to any task-type, a claim that few, if any, would wish to make about any skill. There is, given the link between skill and type of task, a limitedness about skills to the extent that tasks are very often limited types of action, usually involving the accomplishment of a specific and often short-term goal.

Although skills are related to types of task, they also have varying degrees of generality in their application. Just as some task-types are more restricted than others in terms of the range of actions required to accomplish them (the task of governing a country in contrast to the task of tying my shoe-laces), so some skills are more restricted than others in the range of actions that the possessor must perform in order to accomplish them. Thus the skill of reading can be applied to a wide range of texts in the relevant language (although by no means necessarily all of them). Reading typically involves a range of actions which may include matching written symbols to sounds, decoding written symbols, grasping literal meaning, inferring beyond the literal meaning in the text, evaluating what one has understood and enjoying the text, through the entertainment of stimulating thoughts while reading it. By contrast, the skill of chiselling wood can only be applied to certain kinds of wood in certain states so is, in some sense, a less *general* skill than reading, in the sense that it applies to a smaller range of types of task and necessitates a smaller range of actions in order to accomplish such tasks successfully.

The concept of *transferability* is also commonly used in relation to skills, meaning that a skill mastered in one context can be employed in another. Thus, my ability to saw wood in a workshop can be subsequently applied in a forest (perhaps with some modifications to my practice). However, as already noted, it might be objected that there is no real distinction between generality and transferability in skills, since the definition of a type of task might be dependent on context and purpose, so that a skill may appear to be more or less general according to what one is talking about. Thus archery could be defined for some purposes as any kind of shooting with a bow and arrow, or for another, as a skill applied solely to the use of a longbow in an archery contest. And since the ability to shoot a longbow in an archery contest would not necessarily be applicable to say, hunting with a crossbow, it would not be *transferable* to such a context either, so the distinction between generality and transferability appears like a distinction without a difference. Johnson's critical characterization of thinking skills as 'generally transferable' might then be apposite, although it should be noted that Section 7 of his chapter is devoted to general thinking skills. He does not, however, distinguish between general thinking skills and generally transferable thinking skills and we may assume that both authors are happy with the idea that the claim that there are general thinking skills is not significantly different from the claim that there are generally transferable thinking skills.

Nevertheless, although one might not wish to distinguish between general and transferable *skills* might one not wish to distinguish between more and less general kinds of practical ability? To follow up the ability of already discussed ability of a carpenter, it might be said to be more general than that of someone who is merely capable of sawing wood, although both of them may be more or less able to transfer the use of the ability to saw wood from one context to another, from the workshop to the forest for example. In German, this difference in breadth of practical ability is recognized in the language. A *Fähigkeit* in the singular refers, in the context of vocational education, to an integrated occupational capacity with a broad scope (Hanf, 2009). For example, the bricklayer in Germany is considered to be someone who is almost a 'universal construction worker' whose abilities allow him or her to undertake a very wide range of independently conducted activities within the industry. The occupational *Fähigkeit* of a carpenter is not transferable into another occupation like plumbing or plastering, for which a separate vocational education will need to be undertaken.

The individual skills or *Fertigkeiten* of the bricklayer, on the other hand, are narrower in scope but are also potentially *transferable*. For example, the ability to measure length will be useful for bricklaying but for many other activities as well and will, in this sense, be both relatively narrow in terms of the types of action required but, to a considerable degree, transferable.

It is also worth noting one other aspect of broadly conceived abilities like an occupational *Fähigkeit*. A carpenter is expected, not only to carry out the technical activities that are associated with working with wood, but also to plan, co-ordinate and evaluate his or her work. In other words, certain *personal characteristics* are required to successfully practice the occupation of a carpenter, which include being systematic, working considerately and productively with others and having high personal standards. It is an interesting question as to whether or not such individual characteristics, or virtues, are, once acquired, relatively easily transferable to other kinds of activities. A strong tradition of thinking about the virtues would, however, claim that this was the case. If so, it would be the way in which one goes about one's various activities that would be transferable to actions, quite possibly of a completely different type, in other contexts.

It may well be then that the term 'skill' is causing problems of understanding what the term 'thinking skills' actually means. Siegel himself prefers to talk of 'abilities that admit of normative evaluation' rather than skills in this connection (p. 60), leaving it open that thinking abilities are general as well as being possibly transferable, in the sense that they may be quite wide ranging integrative abilities which may involve a range of integrated specific skills, as well as other kinds of know-how. Such an ability may or may not be transferable. To establish that point would require a separate argument which would need to establish that the ability in question could be applied in a wide range of circumstances and/or to a wide range of subject matters. A generally transferable ability would then be broad and integrated and perhaps be related to an activity category such as that of an *occupation*, but would also be capable of application in a range of extra-occupational contexts.

The question would then arise as to whether Johnson's critique of the notion of *thinking abilities* only applies when these are thought of as *thinking skills*. Siegel agrees with Johnson that two connotations of the term 'skill' would be quite inappropriate to all the kinds of abilities that he has in mind. First, in the sense of unthinking, mindless behaviour when presumably a skill is exercised in an almost habitual way. In this sense, insofar as the activity performed scarcely qualifies as an action, it is doubtful whether one can call it the exercise of a skill. Second, it is also clear that for neither author is it acceptable to characterize a thinking skill as nothing more than the exercise of a private and inscrutable mental process. Nevertheless, Siegel's thinking abilities are certainly claimed to be transferable in the sense that they can be used in a variety of contexts and on a variety of different subject matters once acquired in a relatively small number of initial ones. It is plausible to claim also they are general in the sense that they combine and integrate a range of relatively specific skills and other kinds of know-how. Neither does Siegel exclude the possibility that thinking abilities may be more general than skills.

Siegel, as we have seen, does not wish to insist on the term 'skill' to describe the abilities whose existence and usefulness he wishes to defend. To what extent does this blunt Johnson's attack on thinking skills? It may do to the extent that Johnson's critique of thinking skills is focused on the concept of a skill and the reader will notice that Johnson is concerned to make some criticisms of the coherence of the idea that one could apply the concept of a skill to thinking. However, Johnson's principal targets, as Siegel notes, are official initiatives of the governments of England and Wales, Scotland and Northern Ireland. But Siegel wants to maintain that there undoubtedly are thinking abilities. If they are not only skills, then what else might they be? The English word 'skill', as we have already noted, is in some respects difficult to translate into other languages. The home of the concept of skill is located, as we have noted, in manual and co-ordinative dexterities, such as planing, sawing, balancing or archery as they are applied to certain types of tasks. Some people, especially philosophers, tend to get uncomfortable when the concept of a skill is extended beyond these primary contexts. The skill of multiplying in one's head does not arouse too much controversy: we do not find great difficulty with the idea of *mental skills* like this.

Again, some 'social' skills such as knowing how to address a Duke or to eat with a knife and fork at a banquet do not arouse suspicion when classified as skills. What, however, about the so-called 'soft skills' such as being able to relate to other people in formal or informal situations? Is there not a danger of misclassifying them as skills as there seems to be an implicit assumption that, in dealing with other people, we exercise abilities that are qualitatively like those we employ when shaping blocks of wood or damming rivers, namely abilities that are applied to bending inanimate matter to our will? This would seem to be a problem with thinking skills, as they would normally be exercised to no inconsiderable extent on persuading and influencing other people. It is also sometimes thought that skills are value neutral that they can be applied to any objective, evil or good. It is also sometimes thought that the possession of skills has no effect on someone's character. Yet the ability to think clearly and effectively seems to be part of a person's character, just as its absence is also a character trait.

Concerns such as these fuel the idea that the agenda of the proponents of thinking skills is the development of the capacity for technical action uninformed by considerations of value or character development. This is probably one of the factors that motivates Siegel to steer clear of the formulation of his central claims in terms of *skills* as opposed to abilities. He is surely right to see the danger in a formulation of what he wants to claim in terms which either suggest that the ability to engage in generally transferable thinking is value neutral or has no effect on character development. For instance, Siegel is clear that a concern for truth should be central to effective thinking and that certain virtues such as patience and consideration for one's interlocutor and a predisposition towards charitable interpretation of a position are prerequisites of the possessor of sound thinking abilities. In this sense Siegel is no advocate of *sophistry* or the use of argument to gain one's ends no matter what these might be, in the manner of someone like Dionosydorus in Plato's dialogue *Euthydemus* (Plato in Hare and Russell (1970)).

However, it is by no means clear that skills are quite like the philosophical literature often suggests that they are. It seems that skills can be exercised with care, with concern for others, with attention to detail, with a love of excellence and so on. In such cases, we are dealing with the so-called 'bourgeois' (bürgerliche) virtues, described by Kerschensteiner and contrasted with 'civic' (staatsbürgerliche) virtues like courage and generosity (Kerschensteiner 1964). If they are exercised in such a way then it is more difficult to maintain that they are value-neutral. Of course skills can be misused, but so also can virtues more generally. Even the love of justice can arguably be led astray in its exercise by a virtuous person as, for example, Captain Vere in his dealings with Billy Budd in Melville's eponymous novel, or in the misguided actions of a courageous person in a cruel war. Indeed it can be argued that even some skills require civic virtues: the bomb disposal expert requires personal courage but also the ability to appreciate the consequences of his actions on the welfare of other people, for example. If the exercise of skill or at least the skilful performance of tasks involves the development and exercise of virtues, then it is not true to say that the acquisition and the exercise of skills has no effect on the development of a person's character. It is far from clear that a 'skills approach' to thinking or to anything else necessarily isolates the agent either from values or from character development. I would suggest that the problem with the skills in thinking skills is that they are tied to types of task rather than to broader fields of ability, but Siegel appears to recognize that difficulty.

Of course, the common perception that skills have no effect on character or character development may be one that both some of the proponents and some of the opponents of the development of thinking skills may share (for a recent example of this claim about skills, see Hyland 2008). I suspect that the confusion arises because a skill in the sense of a personal attribute is identified with a skill in the sense of a *technique* or way of carrying out a type of task. Since the latter is not a property of any person it is, of course, a mistake to attribute personal characteristics to it. But it is no mistake to attribute personal characteristics to someone's exercise of that technique as skill. If this point is true of skills it is also true of broader abilities.

Of course it is one thing to pay lip service to the recognition of values and to the exercise of virtues in the case of skills, but another thing altogether to have a substantive commitment to the nurture of those values and virtues. But whether or not that is the case will need to be determined by the actual commitments of those who plan and promote 'thinking skills' programmes. Johnson's critique sounds a warning to those who would neglect these aspects of character development in their concern to develop intellectual ability. Johnson does not criticize Siegel over this matter, but as we have noted earlier, Johnson's primary concerns are with proponents of thinking skills within the British educational establishment.

2. Skills and transferability

I want now to look at some actual examples of the transferability of skills in order to see how more uncontroversial cases can be used to understand the claim that 'thinking skills' are generally transferable. A good example is English, where children are asked to make inferences beyond what is literally stated in a text. Given that this content is part of the attainment target of *Reading* in the English part of the English National Curriculum, one may assume that being able to do these things is either a general or a transferable ability or is generally transferable.

As a subject, it has to be taught through the use of a subject matter – one has to be able to read and write about something or other once one has passed the earliest stages. Very often, the early stages of learning to read are based on texts whose primary purpose is pedagogic, to familiarize children with sight-sound (grapheme-phoneme) correspondences and, on the basis of these, to be able, first to *decode* and then to *understand* text. Thus, on a skill of grapheme-phoneme decoding and an associated skill of phoneme blending is built the further skill of decoding, that is of articulating a sound from a written prompt. One can see here how some highly specific skills (namely the extraction of grapheme-phoneme correspondences and the blending of phonemes) are used to develop a slightly more general skill, namely that of decoding, which is relevant to a wider range of written subject matter than pedagogically designed texts. Decoding, still a relative specific skill, can then be transferred to other texts and can be gradually developed to deal with texts of increasing complexity, thus becoming more general in the range of its application. Indeed, it and the earlier, simpler, skills are also *transferable* since, having been acquired through one or more kinds of texts, they can be used in connection with many others. We can see, therefore, that skills may have varying ranges of *generality*, that is, the tasks that they encompass have relatively broad or narrow scope and that they are also *transferable*, that is they can be acquired in one type of task and then used in another, more or less related, task. It is not always the case that a transferable skill is also general. For example, a skill that is only useable in highly specific circumstances in a very particular type of task, like the use of a particular tool to attach or detach a component on the engine of a car could be used in a wide range of circumstances where this task needed to be carried out, perhaps in different kinds of machinery and thus be specific but transferable. However, broader abilities such as mastery of an occupation or, in the example above, that of accomplished reading, may well be characterizable as both general and transferable, general in this context being a relative term, certain abilities are relatively general compared with more specific ones. In this case, the practice of an occupation or advanced reading involves the integrated deployment of many different skills and can then be described as relatively general.

Reading, everyone would agree, is incomplete and of little value unless it involves *understanding* of the text which one is reading. Therefore, one of the abilities that is acquired and developed through the early stages of learning to read is not just the matching of seen to sounded words and chunks of text, but the ability to grasp the sense of what is in the written text. In its most elementary form this involves being able to explain the *literal meaning* of sentences in the text; later it will involve being able to *reorganize* the meaning for a specific purpose, to make *inferences* within and beyond the text, *evaluate* the quality of aspects of the text and to develop *appreciation* of its aesthetic and other qualities (Beard 1990). These abilities may be called skills, but one should be aware of a difference between them and the earlier mentioned skills of decoding. They are relatively broad and arguably unrelated to specific types of tasks as they can be used across an increasing variety of different texts and different kinds of text. They build on and presuppose already existing abilities to reorganize, infer, evaluate and appreciate that have been, and continue to be developed in spoken language and finally their successful development and transfer into application to other texts will depend to no small degree on vocabulary and subject specific knowledge. However, there can be little doubt that the ability to read texts is also *transferable* to other types of tasks or activities to a greater or lesser degree, dependent on an individual's possession of other forms of know-how and propositional knowledge. One could also say that reading, once fluency has been acquired, is a general skill as it is applicable to many different subject matters. In some cases, therefore, such as with reading or 'thinking skills' we may not wish to distinguish between the generality and the transferability of abilities.

Someone might wish to object at this point that it is questionable whether reading is a transferable ability; why not say that a different ability is exercised each time a different text-type is encountered, so that when different forms of know-how (e.g., words with different roots) and different forms of knowledge (e.g., knowledge of hydraulics when reading a plumbing manual) are encountered, then the difference is sufficiently great for us to say that a different kind of reading ability is involved? This move is suggested in Cigman and Davis (2008) when they write:

> Do we understand the notion of a 'specific ability' which is not *simply* an ability to x or y, but is transferable *from x to y*? What reason do we have to say (or indeed deny) that the ability that now manifests as an ability to y is the *same ability* as that which formerly manifested as an ability to x? (Davis and Cigman, 2008, op.cit. p.705)

This quotation suggests that there is a problem about the very notion of transferability. Any ability is an ability of someone to do something or other. Since that something or other is specific (it is, for example, a particular task), it cannot follow that ability to do task A is the same ability the ability to do task B, even if the agent can do both. It would thus not follow from Jones' ability to read *The Lord of the Rings* in English that he possessed the ability to read *The Charterhouse of Parma* (in English). If Jones were able to read both this would indicate that he had manifested two distinct abilities. Notice that this very strong doctrine of non-transferability is not one held by Johnson, who writes:

> . . . Yet in a minimal and trivial sense all skills are transferable in so far as all skills can be repeated in relevantly similar circumstances . . . (p. 20)

a property which Johnson refers to as 'portability' which appears to be similar to 'transferability' as I am using the term in this afterword. The position described in the Davis and Cigman quotation above could be characterized as 'extreme non-transferability'. In this respect Johnson expresses the consensus view about how we are to understand attributions of practical knowledge, namely that they apply to task or activity *types* rather than *tokens* or particular instances. Abilities thus apply to *types* of tasks or activities, although they are *manifested* in particular tasks and activities when they are exercised. An ability that was only applicable to one particular task would not be transferable since, by stipulation, it would be a different ability when exercised on a different task. But there is little warrant in the way in which we talk about skills and abilities for claiming that abilities apply to individual (token) tasks rather than types of task, although there may well be debate about the breadth of a task-type and the range of contexts in which it applies. But this is only to be expected since our language is often vague and purpose- and context-dependent in relation to these issues. But if ability to x is an ability to perform a type of task and if the criteria of identity for a specific task-type are sufficiently recognized, then there is little difficulty in maintaining that the ability to x can be transferred to a range of different situations in which the same task-type can be identified. The ability to decode text in English, for example, can be applied to texts in plumbing, finance and literature. Provided that we understand that ascribing know-how to someone is to ascribe to them an ability to carry out an activity or task of a certain type, then it is relatively unproblematic to talk of the transfer of, for example, a skill exercised on one particular task to another. On this point I take it that there is consensus between Johnson and Siegel.

But talk of transfer can go beyond this, since many activities consist of integrated systems of sub-activities or subskills and a skill involved in one type of more complex ability may be capable of exercise in the same type of task implicated in a different complex activity. In this sense, know-how applicable in one *type of activity* may well be transferable to another type of activity, for example calculation in accountancy to calculation in engineering. Whether it is transferable directly without the acquisition of some further knowledge or know-how is a question that needs to be settled through examination of the detail of each case.

Looking at the analogy between the ability to read and the ability to think, in the case of reading that we are considering, it is far from clear that the ability to infer one sentence from another within a text, or to infer a proposition that is not within the text from one that is, is *generally transferable*, as opposed to a relatively general ability exercisable over a range of cognate subject matters which nevertheless failed to apply to a significant range of other subject matters. Given that one may be able to talk in a fairly confident way about the transferability of some inferential abilities within an *academic subject area*, for example, it does not follow that we can be confident about the transferability of that ability beyond that subject area to another one, or to non-academic contexts. It is in connection with the issue of the transfer of an ability from one type of activity or from one subject area to another that the main points of difference between Johnson and Siegel emerge.

The problems in the case of inferring are compounded in the case of other possible thinking abilities such as *comparing, evaluating* or *creating*. When one compares one thing with another, one does so in some respect or another and with some purpose in mind. The discovery of sameness and difference will depend on what one is comparing and for what purpose one is doing the comparing. In looking for signs of life, the comparison of a living human being with a doll would suggest great dissimilarity; in assessing form and shape, the two might be quite similar, compared with, say a crocodile or a worm. Another consideration is that comparison may require detailed examination and knowledge of the items to be compared, for example for a medical doctor in the examination of healthy and diseased bodily organs. One cannot expect someone to do this without the relevant background know-how and propositional knowledge. For these reasons, and for others Siegel is inclined to agree with Johnson that the ability to compare, thought of either as a general ability of extremely broad scope across different subject matters, or as a relatively specific ability capable of easy transfer to other subject matters, is to be regarded with some suspicion. Siegel does not specify what other supposedly very general abilities might be subject to similar strictures, but one suspects that, where similar considerations to *comparing* apply, he would agree with Johnson.

3. The question of efficacy

What do we know of the efficacy of teaching thinking skills within the National Curriculum? How would one determine whether or not the teaching of thinking skills had been worthwhile? Would it relate to increased learning and understanding within a particular subject, or across more than one subject or would it have broader effects in terms of the learner's growing autonomy? The National Curriculum documentation itself gives little clue as to what it sees as the desirable outcomes of this specific strand of the curriculum, let alone which are more desirable than others. As we have noted, Siegel does not agree that there are universal abilities – abilities that are applicable to any kind of subject matter. He does maintain that there is a set of abilities, broad in scope, which may with relative ease be transferred, once they have been learned, to other subject matters and contexts. It is not entirely clear whether or not Johnson thinks that there are such abilities and, if so, just what they are. Thus it could be the case that Siegel thinks that there are some generally transferable abilities and that Johnson thinks that there are none. More plausibly, they may both agree that there are some generally transferable abilities but disagree *either* about what the set of generally transferable abilities is, or *how* transferable they are, or both. If the latter is the case then the disagreement between the two has to be settled through the detailed discussion of examples and evidence rather than through very general abstract or logical considerations.

Empirical evidence on the efficacy of thinking skills programmes is limited. A useful source is Solon (2007) who reviews the extant literature and reports a small-scale study in which a group of psychology students of similar attainment were divided into a control and an experimental group. The experimental group was given an infusion programme of generic critical thinking instruction and homework while the control group was not. Without detriment to their post-test performance on a psychology test it was found that the experimental group made significant gains on the Cornell Z test as a measure of critical thinking compared with the control group. Solon acknowledges the limitations of a small-scale (not purely experimental) study and the need for further work, but suggests that this study shows that critical thinking can be taught through infusion methods without detriment to subject instruction. More empirical work does certainly need to be done and the results presented here are very interesting, particularly in their report of non-detriment, which is obviously a concern whenever curriculum substitution is mooted.

One may however wonder how to interpret these results as they relate to critical thinking ability. The experimental group received instruction in generic (generally transferable) critical thinking skills and the post-experimental critical thinking instrument, the Cornell Z test, measured ability in generic critical thinking. Thus it was established that instruction in generic critical thinking within the experimental group resulted in statistically significant increases in test scores in critical thinking skills. This would not, however, be sufficient to show that the critical thinking skills thus acquired were *transferable*. One would need to conduct further empirical work to establish this in order to ascertain whether improved critical thinking abilities resulted in improved understanding and performance in a range of subject matters, including the subject matter in which the critical thinking programme had been embedded. So we cannot say at this stage that there has been conclusive evidence for the claims of the advocates of critical thinking skills, although it has become clearer what kind of evidence needs to be collected in order to establish such claims.

4. What is thinking?

The concept of a skill poses problems for those who advocate the development of thinking as a cross-curricular subject. These problems are mainly concerned with the narrowness of skills and the fact that they are related to the performance of tasks rather than to broader types of activity. We want to say (rightly) that thinking is very often concerned with broader categories of activities than tasks, for example with the conduct of one's professional activity as a whole. But these problems can be resolved by refusing to confine thinking to skills and by admitting that the adjective 'thinking' can be applied to broader categories of agency as well as to the performance of highly specific tasks. The term 'thinking' and its cognates have excited far more philosophical attention than 'skills' and much of this debate is, not surprisingly, highly relevant to the issue under consideration in this volume.

Siegel suggests that clarity about thinking abilities is best achieved by pointing to the kind of teaching that might be done which would exemplify teaching general thinking abilities (Siegel, p. 68). This consists of such activities as: identifying unstated assumptions, reconstructing arguments in premise-conclusion form, stating the nature of the relationship between the premises and conclusions, and evaluating the arguments, identifying any particular fallacies. In other words, Siegel maintains, there are perfectly ordinary and straightforwardly intelligible examples of thinking skills, but they do not exclude broader categories of agency. So it is pretty clear what the focus of Siegel's advocacy in respect of thinking skills actually is, as it is largely related to the development of the ability to understand, analyse, criticize and construct arguments. Thinking, then, can relate to particular types of task such as identifying the premises and conclusions of arguments in a particular field, but could be part of a broader activity such as, for example, developing a critical approach to History.

5. Mental processes

What is not so clear, however, is the characterization of these abilities as 'thinking abilities'. Siegel claims that thinking involves mental acts or events of one sort or another and that such events 'all depend on or are manifestations of particular sorts of brain activity' (pp. 67–68). If the activities described above are cases of thinking then it would not necessarily follow that they were either mental (non-physical) events nor manifestations or results of brain activity, even if they were associated with such processes (see Hacker 2007 for example). But is thinking a type of mental event? One point worth noting about the examples above is that they can take place either publicly as part of a discussion in a social context or through the solitary writing out, for example, of sentences with premises at the top of the page and conclusions at the bottom, they can be rehearsed in 'inner speech' or they can be carried out as internal acts of judgement, rather like mental arithmetic calculation. The last case is clearly one where we are inclined to say that the exercise of the ability *involves* mental occurrences, but are the first two or three? All of them are clear examples of intellectual activity, but are they simply examples of sequences of mental events? One could maintain that any outward activity like sequencing an argument on paper needs to be accompanied by a mental sequencing which is a precondition for the one that is done on paper. But again, this is philosophically controversial and is not required by the claim that there are generally transferable abilities of this kind (see Ryle 1949). Neither Johnson nor Siegel seem to be committed by their arguments to any such claim. Whether or not one calls such mental events examples of *thinking* is again not central to the issue under discussion, since they can be described in more specific ways. One might begin to be puzzled as to why the debate about thinking skills has been framed around the concept of thinking, just as one can be puzzled as to why it has been framed around skills, as opposed to performing activities like analysing arguments.

The puzzle is heightened by the realization that one can, for example, evaluate an argument in a thoughtful or a thoughtless manner. Indeed, to the extent that doing so is an instance of exercising a skill, one could be said to do so more or less skilfully to the extent that one did so more or less thoughtfully. At the very least, being thoughtful about evaluating an argument is, other things being equal, more likely to lead to success than not being thoughtful about it. A thoughtful evaluator of arguments will take care to be accurate, consider alternative interpretations, check his interpretation with others and try to understand what the person offering the argument was trying to achieve. One reason why instruction and practice in the carrying out of such activities is advocated is because it is believed that it will make evaluators of arguments more thoughtful and better at what they are doing. This is the kernel, as I understand it, of the claim of advocates of the teaching of 'thinking skills'.

However, if evaluating an argument is an example of thinking (however one wishes to characterize thinking), then it seems that one could think thoughtlessly in the sense that one could fail to do the good things mentioned above. This is not a particularly welcome conclusion, even if it is not necessarily disastrous, for someone who holds that thinking is a mental process, but it does raise the question as to how important it is for the advocate of the teaching of thinking abilities to insist that it involves instruction, training and practice in the exercise of thinking as opposed to, say, argument analysis.

It is worth noticing a divergence between the concepts of thought on the one hand and skill on the other in this respect. It is possible to exercise a skill unskilfully, for example if one is a novice or one is not taking care of what one is doing. We say, for example, that Jones laid the brick wall in an untidy manner. It is also true to say of someone evaluating an argument that they did so inaccurately or in an uncharitable manner. But thinking with little or no thought seems at the least philosophically odd, while exercising a skill in an unskilful manner seems less so. To say that someone analyses arguments carelessly or ineptly, on the other hand, is certainly not odd.

Fortunately, evaluation of the claims of Siegel and other advocates of the teaching of 'thinking skills' does not require the resolution of such issues, as in an important sense the debate between them and their critics depends neither on insisting on a common meaning of the term 'skill' nor of 'thinking'. The debate is rather about whether a particular range of activities is generally transferable or not and clarity is best served by focusing on this question, which is what both authors largely confine themselves to. This strategy has the very welcome consequences of allowing their readers to eliminate distractions and to focus on the substantial issues at stake. It is not clear, therefore, that the debate about thinking skills is about thinking either, as opposed to the generality and transferability of certain kinds of abilities.

6. A summary of Johnson's claims

Johnson's assault on the teaching of thinking skills is focused on the claim that the skills advocated by thinking skills enthusiasts do not exist. Whatever these abilities are, they are poorly characterized as 'skills' and to say that they involve thinking is also problematic, as thinking is too vague or ramified a concept to be associated with a particular kind of activity. Johnson does not deny that people think, nor that some are better at it than others, nor even that one can be assisted through pedagogic means to become better at thinking. The important point at issue is whether or not these abilities have the required general transferability to make it pedagogically worthwhile to devote time and resources to teaching them. On this point, Johnson and Siegel beg to differ. One further point of agreement between the two should be mentioned. Johnson would deny and Siegel certainly does not claim, that there is a *universal* ability of thinking or reasoning which can be applied to any activity. The dispute is over a much more restricted point, which concerns whether or not such abilities are *generally transferable*. Given that universality is excluded the question then rests on a matter of degree. Is there an ability associated with reasoning well which is very broad in scope which applies once one acquires it in a wide range of subject matters, or alternatively, which is, with little or no extra knowledge, transferable into a wide range of subjects, or are there no such abilities?

Johnson denies that there are a range of skills that are generally transferable. These include those set out in the National Curriculum: *creative thinking, enquiry, evaluation, information processing* and *reasoning*. The claim is that there are no such skills or abilities of a general nature which can be identified independently of the subject matters to which they apply or the contexts in which they are exercised. Thus, although it is possible to apply one's ability to evaluate the technique used in painting portraits in oil on successive paintings, it is not possible to apply that ability to evaluate the musical merits of an opera score or the efficiency of a steam engine. His claim would be that these are distinct abilities because the types of activity on which they are exercised have too little in common for it to be possible to identify any substantial element that they have in common with each other which would make it worthwhile to teach in such a way as to promote transfer from one type of activity to another.

It may be doubted whether Johnson is opposed either to the idea that, within particular subject matters, abilities that can best be described as creative thinking, evaluation etc. are desirable attributes and should be cultivated by anyone seeking to be proficient, let alone excellent in the subject that he or she is setting out to master. The claim would rather be that these abilities are specific to the subject being studied and that they have limited, if any, transfer to other areas. Although he does not call on the British philosopher of education, Paul Hirst and his earlier work on *forms of knowledge*, in many ways Hirst's arguments for the distinctiveness of the central concepts, proposition and methods of enquiry in broadly distinct areas of human knowledge would be congenial to the case made out by Johnson (Hirst 1974). The proficient thinker in a particular subject or form of knowledge would, on this account, be someone who had acquired the ability to think effectively through *immersion* in the subject matter, by learning the skill of, say argument analysis through the study of History.

The most popular alternative view to this, set out by McGuiness and quoted in Johnson's contribution, is the *infusion* approach which 'seeks to embed thinking skills within curricular areas by utilising opportunities for developing general thinking skills within curriculum subjects' (Johnson, pp. 5–6). The general abilities are thus developed within curriculum subjects and transferred to others once acquired. Unlike the immersion approach, the target general abilities are explicitly identified and then applied within the subject. Since he denies that there are such general abilities he denies the feasibility of the infusion approach. But, as we have seen, Siegel is, at the very least, cautious about endorsing the existence of a range of abilities such as *comparing*, without examining whether or not these have the generality that some ascribe to them. Without getting our authors to mount a detailed examination of each of these abilities and their possible general transferability it is difficult to establish the precise degree of agreement and disagreement between them on this general issue.

7. Reasoning

However, on one particular issue it appears that there are clear and identifiable differences, namely whether the practice of *argument analysis and evaluation* is a generally transferable ability or one that is of limited or no general transferability. Johnson does not devote his argument explicitly to this type of ability, but one may safely assume that it is one of the many kinds of putative thinking skills that he wishes to deny the existence of.

There are some reasons for thinking that this is a curious place for sharp divisions between the two authors to emerge. After all, few deny that the systematization of arguments is a science that has made significant progress since the time when Aristotle enumerated the forms of syllogistic reasoning and particularly since the work of Gottlob Frege at the end of the nineteenth century made possible the incorporation of some forms of reasoning into formal calculi. Even if we ignore the formalization of reasoning, it is also the case that the informal study of argumentation has been intensively developed and the classifications of fallacies and mistakes in informal reasoning have been widely accepted. Indeed, Johnson himself makes use of them in his arguments against general thinking skills.

The study of informal reasoning is different in scope from the study of its formal counterpart, as a move in a formal calculus may be allowable in that calculus but useless in the everyday context of a discussion or argument. For example, the fallacy of *begging the question*, which involves making either overtly or covertly, an assumption which is also the conclusion or part of the conclusion that one wishes to draw, is generally accepted as a fallacy. Someone who already presupposes what he seeks to argue for in the premises of his argument can scarcely expect the assent of his interlocutor to the argument, since it assumes something that he may not be inclined to accept, which may possibly be the point of dissension in a discussion. On the other hand, an argument one of whose premises is also the conclusion is trivially sound or valid. So the teaching of reasoning will not be confined to a knowledge of and facility with arguments which are sound or which are valid, but will be concerned with whether or not one is entitled or obliged to accept a conclusion as the result of a particular argument.

Since Johnson's case is built on the careful construction of his own arguments it may be asked what the status of these arguments is and what the scope of their application might be. An interlocutor hostile to Johnson may even pose the following dilemma. On the one hand, Johnson's arguments, if they are good ones, are specific to philosophy and cannot be applied to attempts to justify the teaching of reasoning made in other disciplinary contexts such as psychology. On the other hand, if they have a transdisciplinary application are they not examples of the exercise of just the kind of ability that Johnson has devoted much effort to denying the existence of? Johnson identifies four fallacious moves which he maintains that the proponents of thinking skills are guilty of: *reification, essentialism, naming* and *generalization*. Let us examine whether they have the kind of general transferability that could be damaging to Johnson's case.

Reification involves wrongly treating what is referred to by a word or a phrase as a thing, on the analogy of a proper name. Thus, if one describes Jones as engaged in thinking, there must be an activity, namely thinking, in which he is engaged. When it is said that Jones is running, then most would acknowledge, there is a kind of activity, namely running, that Jones is said to be doing. Johnson maintains that it does not follow from the fact that an expression appears to refer to an activity that it does in fact do so, even though there may be apparently related cases where it does. Does Johnson here appeal to a general principle whose existence his argument is concerned to deny, namely a fallacy in reasoning which can be detected across a range of subject matters? On the face of it this looks to be so, but it is also clear that Johnson could mount a defence of his use of the fallacy of reification. Whether one commits the fallacy depends on the particular examples under consideration. While to say that there is an activity of running which Jones is said to be doing when it is asserted that Jones is running is not to commit the fallacy of reification, to say that there is an activity of thinking that Jones is doing when it is asserted that Jones is thinking is to commit that fallacy. Whether or not the fallacy has been committed will depend on careful conceptual analysis of the use of the term which appears to indicate an activity. Whether the surface grammatical form of a verb is misleading us will need to be established by a detailed philosophical investigation of thinking. One might ask, for example, whether the fallacy of reification is being committed when, having noted that Jones is evaluating an argument, there is an activity that Jones is performing, namely evaluating an argument.

A similar point could be made about *essentialism*. One may concede that while a term designating a physical element refers to a structural essence (although this is debatable) it does not follow that a term referring to a human ability refers to a structural essence. Again, it may be maintained, this will need to be argued on the specifics of the case before it can be established that the fallacy of essentialism has been committed. The *naming fallacy* arises, according to Johnson, from the fact that it does not follow that a general term exists that it refers to, for example, a general ability. From the truth of 'Jones is evaluating the applicant's CV' it does not follow that there is a general activity, *evaluating* that he is currently engaging in. Again, whether or not an activity is relatively broad or relatively narrow in scope is one that needs to be considered on its merits, it is not one that can be settled in general. Arguably therefore, as in the cases of the other alleged fallacies, it can be maintained that Johnson is appealing to the need for conceptual investigation in detail rather than to a generally transferable principle.

Finally, there is what Johnson calls the *generalizing fallacy*. If one knows how to open a tin it does not follow that one knows how to open things. First, because there is not necessarily any general activity of *opening* that can be applied to all sorts of different objects and secondly because it is false to conclude of some property that applies to a specific type of instance (... is able to open a can) that it can be applied to a range of types of activity (... is able to open an X). While it is possible to say that the first aspect of this fallacy needs to be investigated in detail before we can accuse anyone of committing it, the second aspect of it looks like an instance of a much more general principle that we would recognize as having a wide application, namely that what is true of one type of task is not necessarily true of all types of tasks. In this sense then, Johnson might be considered to be appealing to an ability to identify a particular fallacy that is applicable over a wide range of contexts and is valid in a wide range of subject matters.

8. The role of philosophy

Johnson and Siegel largely, although by no means exclusively, deploy philosophical arguments in support of their positions. Philosophical techniques such as conceptual analysis (to which both authors are committed), are thought to be applicable across a range of different subject matters. Conceptual analysis involves detailed investigation of the ways in which concepts are used, preferably without preconceptions as to what such an investigation might yield. Furthermore, even analytically minded philosophers disagree about the nature and even the purpose of conceptual analysis. However, the very fact that the potential scope of conceptual analysis is very broad and the fact that the techniques involved, although often specialized, are applicable to a wide range of contexts, makes it look like a kind of 'thinking skill' that might be of considerable use. Don't we have, then, an argument for the teaching of a certain kind of philosophy as a set of techniques of wide applicability? If this is the case then perhaps Johnson and Siegel could agree on a philosophy syllabus that could be used within the secondary stage of education alongside the more traditional subjects. It would not involve the positing of such vague and somewhat vacuous general abilities such as being creative, comparing, evaluating etc., but would focus on the virtues of clear, detailed and systematic thinking. Johnson acknowledges this but points out that successful philosophical engagement involves detailed knowledge of the area under consideration. It is no good debating aesthetics if one has no knowledge of or feeling for works of art for example. Nevertheless, since both Siegel and Johnson could sign up to this proposition we could urge them to consider whether or not philosophy could have a role on the secondary curriculum alongside other well-established subjects which would provide some of the detailed subject knowledge necessary for effective philosophical reflection.

9. Reason and argument

We saw that the case that Siegel really wanted to defend was that of the efficacy of argument analysis (and, presumably, synthesis). The ability to construct and to deconstruct arguments would, for him, be a prime and very valuable example of a thinking ability that should be cultivated in the school and college curriculum. It is not being suggested that one can reason effectively without having a good grasp of the subject matter under consideration. The claim made is rather that *given* good subject knowledge and given acquisition of the ability to analyse and synthesize arguments, learning can, other things being equal, take place more effectively with the latter in addition than with the former alone. Is this contestable?

In order to address the question it is necessary to ask what an argument is. Here we straightaway encounter an ambiguity. In one sense an argument is a kind of conversational encounter that articulates difference of opinion between one or more people in which one party attempts to persuade the others that they should hold a certain belief on the basis of certain reasons. In order to make sense of and evaluate the claims made by different parties who engage in such conversational activities, it is frequently necessary to render their claims and the supporting reasons for those claims in a structured form, in which the claim offered is identified as the *conclusion*, the beliefs which are appealed to as starting point are the *premises* and the steps between premises and conclusion as the *intermediate steps* (there may or may not be any of these). Such structures of propositions, whereby conclusions are supported by premises and intermediate steps are also called 'arguments'. Different structures will emerge from such attempts. At their simplest, they will reveal an argument within an ongoing conversation or discussion whose various stages are punctuated by the challenges of an interlocutor, whose objections then have to be addressed. In more complex situations one may well find two rival arguments being offered within an ongoing discussion or conversation.

The situation is usually more straightforward in formal genres such as making a speech because the structure of the argument is made relatively clear. The same goes for arguments set out in written form. But since most arguments are presented in everyday conversational life, the ability to recognize, extract and evaluate arguments is an important social and cognitive ability or family of abilities.

Afterword

Argument analysis will, then involve extraction of the arguments from spoken exchanges or from passages of text where this is necessary, followed by an evaluation of whether or not they support their conclusions (bearing in mind that this is not merely a matter of formal validity – see below). However, this is likely to be a complicated business which involves a range of abilities and attitudes which are often hard to maintain in complex and sometimes conflict-ridden situations. Nevertheless, it is plausible to maintain that such abilities and attitudes may be of considerable value in all aspects of our lives, ranging from the domestic to the vocational and, in the context of the educational aim of autonomy, to be highly prized.

However, Argument Analysis (in which I include Argument Identification) is a complicated matter. This is for a number of reasons:

(1) Conversations or written texts often do not fully articulate the arguments that are embedded in them, for reasons of brevity, competitiveness and the taking for granted of background assumptions.
(2) It is one thing to ascertain that there is an argument embedded within a discussion or a text; it is another to determine what the nature of that argument is and to secure agreement with one's interlocutor(s) what the nature of that argument is.
(3) There is often considerable disagreement about how arguments should be analysed, which includes disagreement about *what kind of arguments* they are.

Point (1) may not necessarily be a problem for Argument Analysis, so much as one of its main teaching objectives. Indeed, Siegel makes it clear that locating hidden premises (and presumably hidden intermediate steps) in arguments is precisely something that someone committed to teaching thinking skills should be concerned to develop. Nevertheless, the ability to do so may well depend on considerable detailed knowledge of the subject area under consideration. This does not necessarily put the infusion approach under pressure but indicates that there is not necessarily any short cut to inferential ability within a subject matter without a thorough acquaintance with that subject matter.

Point (2) raises more complex issues. It is likely to be the case that a discussion about the quality or otherwise of an argument presented may change into a discussion about *which* argument is being presented. On one interpretation an argument may be a good one, on another it may not. How one characterizes an argument may, then, be a complex issue not subject to a ready resolution. This may be a technical issue to do with how one should interpret certain complex sentences for example, it may be to do with the identification of implicit premises, or it may be to do with one interlocutor's willingness or otherwise to give the benefit of the doubt to a co-disputant in the interpretation of the argument.

In most cases, arguments are evaluated in respect of their *form* or their structural characteristics. This means that one has to identify the form under which the argument is offered.

Point (3) raises a further and more complex issue which is closely related to point (2). This concerns the extent to which it is possible to identify the form of the argument independently of the subject matter with which it is concerned. The form of an argument is obtained by removing phrases from some of the constituent phrases of the argument and substituting variable letters for them. Two or more arguments that share the same form will be equally as bad or as good as each other in terms of providing a justification of the conclusions on the basis of the premises. This may seem like an abstruse point but it is of importance in the most ordinary contexts of argument evaluation.

Take a famous example of the analysis of everyday reasoning, one of the encounters between Larry and Charles M in a recording of a street corner discussion related by Labov (1969). Simplifying slightly, the position is this. Larry asserts that

> An when people be sayin' if you good you goin' to heaven an' if you bad you goin' to hell, that's bullshit. Good or bad you goin' to hell anyway.

It has been argued, for example by Cooper (1984), that Larry has implicitly contradicted himself by asserting first that it is false that if you are bad that you are going to hell and then saying that good or bad, you are going to hell, in which case if you are bad you are going to hell. But it can be argued that Larry is denying the whole sentence not each of its parts. He is not saying that it is false that if you are good then you are going to heaven and it is false that if you are bad then you are going to hell, but rather saying that the whole story of the form 'if you are good then you are going to heaven and if you are bad you are going to hell' is false. To adapt the language of logicians the 'bullshit' operator has, as its scope the whole conjunctive sentence, it is not applied separately to each of its conjuncts. And if this is so, Larry is consistent. He asserts that the whole story is false and makes an alternative, non-contradictory claim. Whether or not this argument is about the afterlife or about anything else, it is as good or as bad as the form under which it is offered. Siegel would probably wish to say that the interlocutor of someone offering such an argument *if he wants to understand him* is bound to adopt the interpretation which is most likely to make the argument being offered a good one rather than a bad one. The problem might be, however, that even with a good disposition it may actually be quite difficult to identify just what the form of the argument is.

As it turns out, on one charitable interpretation Larry's complete argument can be shown to be *formally valid*. It is, on this reading, an argument whose validity does not depend on the inferential potential of terms related to any particular subject matter like 'heaven' or 'hell', but on terms that occur in any subject matter: 'and', 'not', 'if . . . then . . . ' etc. Arguments offered under such a form never lead from true premises to false conclusions. It does thus seem as if at least some of the arguments offered in the course of everyday discussions seem to depend on non subject-specific logical considerations. It would be natural to assume that someone with the appropriate training in logic, and with the appropriate set of dispositions for engaging in argument analysis would be able to evaluate arguments offered in many different subject matters. On this account it would seem that Siegel's version of Thinking Skills would have some educational value, since if this example is at all representative, non-subject specific reasoning skills have an application.

Unfortunately, and not surprisingly matters, are not that simple. Not all arguments can be assessed for their formal validity or invalidity. This remains the case even when such arguments can be classified as *deductive*, when their validity requires that the truth of their premises is incompatible with the falsity of their conclusions. Thus

> This brick is red all over
> Therefore,
> This brick is not green

is valid because it cannot be the case that it is true that this brick is red and false that it is not green. We understand the inference, however, because of our grasp of the inferential relationships that hold between words expressing colour concepts. More generally, it is plausible to say that many arguments have this feature, whether their subject matter is specialist or non-specialist. And, if that is so, instruction in how to identify and evaluate arguments that, when put forward are claimed to be formally valid in the sense outlined above, will be as useful as the number of arguments of this kind are prevalent. The answer to this question is that we do not know. One way of responding to this claim is to suggest that the argument above contains a suppressed premise:

> Anything that is red all over is not green

so that the whole Argument will read:

> Anything that is red all over is not green
> This brick is red all over
> Therefore,
> This brick is not green

which makes it a formally valid deductive argument.

It is highly questionable, however, that we learn to handle the conceptual relationships within a field such as colour concepts in this way. We do not notice that nothing that is red all over is also green by observing lots of red things, and inductively concluding the truth of the major premise, but by grasping the conceptual relationships within the field of colour concepts through being taught how to use colour concepts and then using them ourselves. If it were nothing more than a matter of observation then we may be continually waiting for an example of something red all over to be green as well in order to determine whether we could be certain that the argument proved the conclusion. But anyone who held this or who acted as if it were true would be rightly considered not to have obtained a comprehensive grasp of the field of colour concepts. This suggests that the principle of inference that leads us from

> This brick is red all over
> to
> This brick is not green

is the rule of inference which applies in the field of colour concepts to the effect that nothing that is red all over is, or can be, green. Therefore, our grasp of this inference and of many other subject-dependent inferences is not wholly or partly dependent on formal logical laws but on material subject dependent inferences, where it is the inferential relationships between, in this example, colour concepts that is important, not the 'logical operators' such as 'not . . .', '. . . and . . .' or 'if . . . then . . .'. Knowing the syllogistic form that makes the argument above with the extra premise valid will not generally help someone to handle arguments that involve a grasp of colour concepts if that person does not already have a grasp of those concepts. If he does, grasp of the syllogistic form will not make him any more adept in handling those types of arguments.

However, Siegel gives us no reason to suppose that the development of reasoning abilities that apply across subjects is dependent on the ability to convert material mode inferences to formal mode ones. His interest seems to lie in the teaching and development of principles that apply equally well to formal and material mode arguments.

10. Inductive arguments

However, many arguments are *inductive* rather than *deductive*. It is possible for this type of argument to be good (sound) but for it to have true premises and a false conclusion, although to the degree that the argument is in fact sound this possibility will be reduced. Some also hold that inductive arguments are also *context sensitive*, meaning that the subject matter with which they deal can affect their degree of soundness or unsoundness. This is because the degree of risk that one is prepared to tolerate in moving from true premises to false conclusions will vary from one subject matter to another. For example, although the following argument is usually taken to be sound, the one following it is not:

> 99 per cent of the apples from the barrel are not rotten.
> This apple is from the barrel.
> Therefore, this apple is not rotten.

because the risks to one's health in moving from true premises to a false conclusion are relatively small, this is not the case with

> 99 per cent of Ruritanian Airways flights reach their destination.
> F666 is a Ruritanian Airways flight.
> Therefore, F666 will reach its destination.

Because the risk to one's health that follows from a false conclusion if one is considering taking the flight is not acceptable.

Inductive arguments also have a property that logicians call *non-monotonicity*, that is their soundness is affected by the addition of new premises. For example,

> 0.0001 per cent of the population were asked about their voting intentions at the next general election.
> 51 per cent of these said that they intend to vote Conservative.
> Therefore, the Conservatives will win the next general election.

is, on the face of it, unsound inductive argument. If, however, we add the premise

> The 0.0001 per cent asked were a random stratified sample of the electors.

to the argument above, we would be inclined to accept the argument as sound. This suggests that filling in more of the context has a significant bearing on the soundness or otherwise of an argument and that, therefore, knowledge of context and of subject matter is a factor affecting our ability to assess the soundness of inductive arguments.

This may seem like a decisive point in favour of the subject dependence of reasoning skills and hence of the necessity of teaching subject principles prior to the teaching of transferable reasoning principles. In this sense the pervasive nature of inductive arguments seems to count in favour of Johnson's thesis and against Siegel's. This would, however, be too quick a response, since even though inductive reasoning is both pervasive in terms of the range of subject matters in which it is used and inductive arguments are also, it is argued, to a degree dependent on the subject matter under consideration for their soundness, it does not follow either that there are *no* subject independent principles of inductive reasoning *nor* that they cannot be taught. Indeed, the existence of textbooks (e.g., Salmon 1984; Hacking 2001) that deal with the principles of inductive logic count against this claim.

Just as it would be wrong to think that Siegel holds that one cannot apply generic reasoning skills to arguments in the material mode, so it would also be wrong to think that he holds this of inductive arguments.

11. Concluding remarks

Having narrowed down the differences of opinion between Johnson and Siegel on the existence of thinking skills and the efficacy of teaching them to differences concerning (largely) the existence of context and subject independent principles of reasoning and the pedagogical efficacy of teaching them, it will now be helpful to see where matters stand in relation to their respective claims.

(1) There is good evidence that context and subject independent argumentation is used in everyday as well as in specialist contexts. What we do not know with any precision is how prevalent the use of such forms of argumentation is.
(2) It is also clear that there is widespread use of subject-dependent deductive reasoning in everyday contexts although again it is not clear to what extent this is the case.
(3) The use of inductive argumentation is very widespread.

The debate seems to be about, not so much whether such forms of argument exist, but rather about their frequency and about whether, to the extent that there are subject-independent principles of reasoning (and both Johnson and Siegel seem to be agreed that there are), it is pedagogically productive to devote time and effort to teaching them rather than something else. It is hard to see how this could be a purely philosophical or conceptual question rather than one to which some of the answers at least will come from empirical research. However, this is an important result and one which has been arrived at through patient philosophical argument which can itself clear the way to framing the kinds of investigations which may or may not lead to further curriculum development. The arguments of neither of the two authors in this volume, however, warrant the wholesale introduction of thinking skills programmes without a very careful consideration of their scope and limits and the evidence of their success in small-scale studies.

References

Beard, R. (1990), *Developing Reading 3-13*, London: Hodder.

Cigman, R. and Davis, A. (2008), 'Commentary (on Section 6, Learners, Teachers and Reflection)', *Journal of Philosophy of Education, Special Issue on New Philosophies of Learning*, 42, 3–4: 705–707.

Cooper, D. (1984), 'Labov, Larry and Charles', *Oxford Review of Education*, 10, 2: 177–192.

Hanf, G. (2009), *National Report on German Vocational Education and Training*, http://www.kcl.ac.uk/schools/sspp/education/research/projects/eurvoc.html

Johnson, S. (2010), *Teaching Thinking Skills*, in Winch, C. (ed.) *Teaching Thinking Skills*, London, Continuum.

Hacker, P. M. S. (2007), *Human Nature: The Categorial Framework*, Oxford: Blackwell.

Hacking, I. (2001), *An Introduction to Probability and Inductive Logic*, Cambridge: Cambridge University Press.

Hare, R. M. and Russell, D. A. (eds) (1970), *The Dialogues of Plato*, Volume 2, London: Oxford University Press.

Hirst, P. (1974), *Knowledge and the Curriculum*, London: Routledge.

Hyland, T. (2008), 'Reductionist Trends in Education and Training for Work: Skills, Competences and Work-Based Learning' in P. Gonon, K. Kraus, J. Oelkers, S. Stolz (eds), *Work, Education and Employability*, Bern: Peter Lang, pp. 129–146.

Kerschensteiner, G. ([1901] 1964), 'Staatsbürgerliche Erziehung für der deutschen Jugend' in *Ausgewählte Pädagogische Texte*, Band 1, Paderborn: Ferdinand Schöningh.

Labov, W. (1969), 'The Logic of Non-Standard English', in Giglioli, P-P. (ed.) (1972) *Language and Social Context*, London, Penguin, pp. 179-215.

Ryle, G. (1949), *The Concept of Mind*, London: Hutchinson.

Salmon, W. (1984), *Logic* (3rd Ed.), Englewood Cliffs, NJ: Prentice Hall.

Solon, T. (2007), 'Generic Critical Thinking Infusion and Course Content Learning', *Journal of Instructional Psychology*, June 2007, pp. 95–109.

Index

abilities that admit of normative evaluation 60, 92
Advanced Level Subject 2, 40
aims of education xi, xiii, 5, 11–12, 21, 66, 99
analyzing
Anderson, J. R. 15, 16, 47, 50
Anselm of Canterbury 20
appreciate, appreciating xi, 9, 10, 15, 37, 38, 39, 45, 46, 56, 95, 98
argument analysis 106, 108, 109, 113, 115, 117
assumptions 46, 52, 62, 65, 66–75, 77–8, 104, 115

Bailin, Sharon 22, 48, 60, 80, 83
Bailin, Sharon; Siegel, Harvey 22, 83
Barrow, Robin 10, 47
Baumfield, V. 27, 35, 36, 47, 49
begging the question 110
Beyer, B. 27, 47
Bobbitt, F. 18, 48
Brain-based Approaches 6

character 8, 54, 55, 66, 94–6
Chase, W. G. 30
Cigman, Ruth 98, 99, 123
Cognitive Acceleration through Science Education (CASE) 5
Cognitive Intervention 6
Coles, A. 26
comparing 26–8, 33, 76, 77, 101, 109, 113

computer model of thought 42, 81, 82
conclusion 33, 36, 40, 67–70, 73
Cooper, David 117, 123
Cornell Z test 102, 103
Cottrell, S. 26–8, 34, 35, 48
counter-examples 59, 75
critical reasoning xii, xiii
creativity 17, 25, 82
curriculum, including English National Curriculum vii, xiii, xiv, xv, xvi, 2, 3, 4, 6, 9, 17, 18, 24, 25, 33, 42, 43, 44–6, 52–4, 83, 96, 101–2, 107–8, 113, 122,

Davis, Andrew vii, 15, 48, 98, 99, 123
De Bono, Edward 6, 13, 21, 27, 29, 33, 38, 39, 48, 59, 81
Dearden, Robert 35, 45, 48
deductive argument 118
Department for Education and Skills (DfES) 3
domain specific knowledge 71–3
Dreyfus, Herbert 31, 48
Dreyfus, Stuart 31, 48

Empson, W. 42, 48
Ennis, Robert 39, 48, 74, 83
enquiry xv, 5, 45, 107–8
essentialism 21, 63, 66, 110, 111
evaluation xv, 4, 5, 42–3, 45, 60, 83, 92, 106–9, 115–16
Evans, J. St. B. T. 30, 48

Index

faculty psychology 13, 16, 17, 25, 63
Fähigkeit 91
Fallacy 21–2, 24–5, 28–9, 33, 36, 61, 63–8, 74–5, 78, 110–12
   Post hoc ergo propter hoc 61
Fertigkeit 91
Feuerstein, R. 6, 18, 33
Fisher, Robert 5, 7, 26, 46, 48, 49
formally valid 117, 118

generalizability 25, 53, 82
generalizing fallacy 24, 25, 29, 36, 63, 74, 112
Goodman, Nelson 14, 49
government xv, 1–3, 5–6, 30, 42, 43, 47, 52, 93

Hacker, P. M. S. 104, 123
Hacking, Ian 121, 123
Hanf, Georg 91, 123
Hare, William 77, 83, 123
Higgins, Stephen 35, 36, 49
Hirst, Paul 108, 123
Hunt, G. M. K. 31, 49
Hyland, Terry 95, 123
hypothesizing 5, 53, 54, 59

imagining, imagination 28, 16, 17, 31, 79, 82
immersion 108, 109
inductive argument 120–2
inferring xv, 64, 89, 101
information processing xv, 5–6, 10, 18–19, 30, 56–7, 63, 107
infusion 5, 6, 74, 102, 108, 109, 115, 123

James, William 16, 49, 61
Johnson, Stephen vii, xi, xiv, xv, xvi, 52–84
Jones, H. M. 40, 56, 49

Kerschensteiner, Georg 94, 123
Knowing how, know-how 10, 24, 56, 93, 92, 98, 100, 101

knowledge 110, 113
Kripke, Saul 14, 49, 63
Kuhn, Herman 34

Labov, William 116, 123
Lave, Jean 15, 49
Learning how to learn xiii, xiv
Lipman, Matthew 6, 33
logic 41, 50, 117, 121, 123
logical thinking xiv, 40

mastery of a subject xiv
material inference 119–21
McGuinness, Carol 3, 6, 7, 13, 14, 27, 34–6, 39, 41, 44, 49, 62, 76, 79, 81, 108
   report 3–7, 18, 25, 27, 30–2, 39, 42, 53, 56, 59–61, 74, 83
McPeck, John 49, 50, 66, 68, 69, 71–4
Mental processes 2, 7, 10, 19, 28–31, 53, 56–60, 78–80, 104
metacognition 5, 45, 49
Miller, D. W. 40

Nabokov, V. 27
National Curriculum xv, 2, 4, 9, 42, 43–5, 50, 52–4, 83, 96, 101, 107
National Strategy 4, 48
   Key Stage Three 4
   Primary 4
Norris, Stephen 21, 65

Oakeshott, Michael 42, 44
onetcenter 19

pedagogic efficacy 11, 13,
pedagogy 23
Perkins, D. N. 16
philosophical approaches 6
Philosophy 33, 46, 47, 59, 68, 110, 112, 113
Plato 94
portability 14, 99
Pratzner, F. C. 36

premise 40, 67–70, 73, 75, 104, 105, 110, 114–21
problem solving 5, 19, 21, 25, 30, 65, 75

Qualifications and Curriculum Authority (QCA) vii, 24, 25, 45
Quinn, Victor 40

reading 73, 89, 90, 96–8, 100
reasoning xii, xv, 16, 24, 26, 28, 30, 38, 46, 54, 64–5, 67, 69–71, 74, 77, 107, 109–12, 116, 118, 120–2
reification 20, 63, 64, 110, 111
Robinson, W. D. 26
rule-following 41, 63, 81
Ruthven, K. 17
Ryle, Gilbert 7, 19, 22, 67, 105

Salmon, Wesley 121
Scheffler, Israel 9, 10, 56, 78, 82
Schwartz, R. and Parks, D. 33
Scriven, Michael 14, 62
Siegel, Harvey xi, xiv, xvi, 22–4, 60, 66, 67, 69, 75, 80, 81, 83, 85, 86, 89, 92–6, 100–2, 104–7, 109, 112, 113, 116–18, 120–2
Simon, H. A. 30
Singley, M. K. 15, 16
skills
general and/or transferable xii, 3, 12, 13, 15, 18, 19, 22, 36, 38, 49, 62, 63, 74, 79, 90
intellectual
Smith, R. 33, 43
Socrates 39
Solon, Tom 102
specialist and subject-specific knowledge xii, 30, 31, 34, 36–7, 46, 51

Sternberg, R. J. 19, 20
subject xiv, xv, xvi, 2, 4, 5, 6, 14, 16, 26, 27, 31, 36–7, 39, 40, 43–6, 48, 52, 54, 62, 67, 68–70, 72, 74–83, 86, 92, 96, 98, 100–3, 107–9, 111, 113–22
subjectivism 35
Suits, Bernard 67

task 15, 16, 24, 25, 29, 32, 74, 88–90, 93, 95, 97–100, 103, 104, 112
task-type 89, 99, 100
technique viii, 19, 31, 38, 45, 89, 95, 108, 112, 113
Thinking through History project 5, 49
truth 2, 7, 9, 31, 34–41, 44–5, 52, 81, 83, 94, 112, 118–19

understand, understanding xi, xiii, xv, 9, 10, 13, 14, 28, 29, 31, 41, 44, 45, 52, 56–60, 62, 79, 92, 96, 97, 101, 103, 104, 117
universal, universality 89, 91, 102, 107

value 3, 33, 35, 36, 38, 39, 43, 44, 46, 81, 94, 95
value-neutral 38, 81, 94
Van den Brink-Budgen, Roy 43
virtue 8, 9, 31, 36, 38, 39, 45, 54–6, 79, 81, 91, 94, 95, 113

Wenger, Etienne 15, 49
Whitehead, Alfred North 47
Wilson, V. 43
Wittgenstein, Ludwig 14, 22, 63, 67